Ibiza

and Formentera

Berlitz Publishing Company, Inc.

Princeton Mexico City Dublin Eschborn Singapore

400 Alexander Park, Princeton, NJ, 08540 USA
9-13 Grosvenor St., London, W1X 9FB UK

Text:	Jack Altman
Editor:	Richard Wallis
Photography:	Jack Altman pages 5, 6, 10, 19, 22, 28, 33, 36, 39, 43, 46, 62, 66, 79, 81, 84; Jon Davison pages 3, 4, 9, 15, 16, 24, 27, 51, 53, 54, 57, 59 (bottom), 61, 69, 75, 76, 88
Cover Photo:	Jon Davison
Photo Editor:	Naomi Zinn
Layout:	Media Content Marketing, Inc.
Cartography:	Ortelius Design

The author wishes to thank Teresa Campillo Torres, Ibiza Island Tourist Office.

Although the publisher tries to insure the accuracy of all the information in this book, changes are inevitable and errors may result. The publisher cannot be responsible for any resulting loss, inconvenience, or injury. If you find an error in this guide, please let the editors know by writing to Berlitz Publishing Company, 400 Alexander Park, Princeton, NJ 08540-6306.

ISBN 2-8315-6967-2
Revised 1999 – Second Printing August 2000

Printed in Italy
020/008 RP

CONTENTS

- A ☛ in the text denotes a highly recommended sight

Ibiza
and Formentera

THE ISLANDS AND THEIR PEOPLE

The miracle of Ibiza is that its fantastic ongoing success with both the Beautiful and not-so-Beautiful People has not hurt its legitimate claim to being simply a beautiful island. While some come just to party all day, all night, the island has many other things to offer. Together with its little neighbor Formentera, Ibiza belongs administratively to Spain's province of Baleares. Commonly known as the Balearic Islands *(Islas Baleares)*, the province also includes Majorca and Menorca and faces Spain's east coast between Barcelona and Valencia.

Ibiza's coastline varies, with long curving stretches of fine sand (great both for beach parties and family enjoyment) alternating with smaller secluded rocky coves and fjord-like inlets for quieter pleasures. Coastal waters are kept clean by stringently enforced antipollution laws.

The resort towns do indeed boast every imaginable disco and bar, each trying to rise higher on the island's own seismic scale of outrageous extravagance. Yet it is always possible to escape to a classic Mediterranean landscape (now well protected by environmental laws) abundant in olive, fig, almond, juniper, palms (to remind us that North Africa is closer than Barcelona), and — above all — shady groves of pine. The profusion of these trees prompted the Greeks to call Ibiza and Formentera the "Isles of Pines," a name the Spanish retained as *Islas Pitiusas*. For a perfect view of these natural beauties as well as the Spanish mainland, drive up to the top of Mount Sa Talaia, which at 475 m (1,558 ft) is the island's highest spot.

Partygoers too exhausted to ramble along clifftop paths or through the wooded wilderness of the interior can hunker down with more peaceful folk in one of the many old inland villages that have retained their traditional charm. Here you are most likely to hear people speaking Ibicenco, the island's dialect, which is related to the Majorcan branch of the Catalan language. In a bar or café across from a gleaming white church and a couple of shops selling straw baskets and terracotta vases, you can sip *hierbas,* an aromatic liqueur distilled from local herbs.

On the Right Track

The islanders' own dialect, Ibicenco, reflects their multiple origins. It has connections with Latin (from the Romans), Arabic (from North African settlers), and the dominant Catalan language (from their historic rulers on the Spanish mainland). Place names are often signposted in Ibicenco rather than Castilian Spanish: Eivissa (Ibiza) or Sant Antoni (San Antonio).

The following list of terms useful to visitors should help keep you on the right track. Castilian Spanish words are provided with their local Ibicenco equivalents.

English	*Castilian/Ibicenco*	*English*	*Castilian/Ibicenco*
palace	*palacio/palau*	quarter	*barrio/barri*
boulevard	*paseo/passeig*	river	*río/riu*
bridge	*puente/pont*	square	*plaza/plaça*
street	*calle/carrer*	cape	*cabo/cap*
cave	*cueva/cova*	church	*iglesia/església*
road	*carretera/ carretera*	harbor	*puerto/port*
		beach	*playa/platja*
avenue	*avenida/avinguda or vía/via*	town hall	*ayuntamiento/ ajuntament*

For many, the ideal refuge from the bustle of Ibiza is its diminutive island neighbor to the south, Formentera. Although Ibiza is small, with an area of 572 sq km (220 sq miles) and 80,000 residents, Formentera is truly tiny: It has a population of barely 5,000 living on just 82 sq km (32 sq miles). It lies only one hour away by ferry and 25 minutes by hydrofoil. Painters love it. Economically poorer than Ibiza, it holds on more firmly to its traditions. The peasant women still wear black. Old stone housing is restored from generation to generation rather than razed and replaced by concrete. Its beaches are less accessible, less crowded. Farther afield, you will find even more idyllically secluded beaches on other, much tinier isles, some of them scarcely more than a rocky outcrop topped by a tree or two, particularly off Ibiza's wilder west coast.

Far from the madding crowd, a peaceful mountain home in Serra de la Mala Costa.

This is not to say you should spend your whole time running away from what gives Ibiza its distinctive character. Ibiza remains very much a festive island of the jet set. But it also lures some of the more modest successors to the hippies of the 1960s who gave Ibiza its modern fame — or notoriety, depending on your taste. And the island boasts (in all senses of the word) a gay community. Wealthier visitors have added swimming pools and tennis courts to tastefully restored farmhouses *(fincas).* They have also built in the inland hills their own handsome white villas in the traditional rounded cubic style introduced centuries ago by Arab landowners.

Resolutely democratic, Ibiza welcomes all sorts to its bars and discos and to the midnight-to-dawn beach raves that make no distinction between penniless and privileged. The island's freewheeling attitude to life is epitomized by the name for its own designer fashion and hairstyles — "Ad-Lib" — coined in those heady 1960s and still going strong. As the place to be for the nightlife, which reaches a crescendo from around 3am with no diminuendo till dawn, Ibiza

Ibiza's local produce is excellent — here, tantalizing offers on display at a Sant Antoni market.

Town has to compete with equally boisterous satellites out at Sant Antoni and Santa Eulària, conveniently linked by an all-night "Discobus" shuttle service running every 30 minutes.

In Ibiza Town the cathedral, convents, and museums inside the walled citadel of Dalt Vila rise above the bars and bistros lining La Marine on the harborside and the boutiques and vegetable market in the narrow streets of La Penya. The east-coast resort of Santa Eulària adds "del Riu" to its name in honor of the island's only river (running just west of the town center) and boasts an imposing fortress-church overlooking the attractive harbor and marina. Busiest of the tourist towns is the ever-growing Sant Antoni (San Antonio in Castilian), with highrise hotels mushrooming up around a magnificent bay and a revered parish church attracting pilgrims to the heart of the town center.

Archaeology buffs can seek out the prehistoric monoliths near Santa Eulària or on Formentera. There are also sites of early Carthaginian settlements: the Grotto of Es Cuieram north of Sant Vicent (where diggers uncovered statues of fertility goddesses) and Ibiza Town's Carthaginian necropolis of Puig des Molins. Or you can simply study the ancient relics in the capital's two archaeology museums.

The Mediterranean climate means no great extremes of temperature. Days are warm throughout the year, but even the heat of high summer is usually tempered by sea breezes. The island's agriculture thrives on its exceptional underground water resources. Vegetables and fruit — olives, apricots, figs, grapes, almonds, oranges, and lemons galore — arrive fresh on your table. In addition to the local seafood, pork and lamb prepared with the island's herbs can be a savory delight. Ibiza is a place for hedonists.

A BRIEF HISTORY

Circles of stone megaliths dating back to 1600 B.C. are the earliest traces of human life on Ibiza and Formentera. Two monumental sites were probably funerary in origin. The better preserved of these is located on Formentera at Ca Na Costa. The other has been excavated on a coastal Ibiza hillside at Cap d'Es Librell, south of Santa Eulària. Rock paintings from 800 B.C. have been found at Ses Fontanelles, near Sant Antoni.

Little else is known of Ibiza's prehistoric inhabitants. The Mediterranean world appears to have ignored the island until its freshwater springs made it a popular stopover for Phoenician seamen plying the route between the European mainland and North Africa.

The Carthaginians

Sailing from their great ports of Tyre and Sidon (modern Lebanon's Soûr and Saïda), the enterprising Phoenician traders founded the city of Carthage on the Tunisian coast in the ninth century B.C. Two hundred years later they set up colonies on Ibiza, whose name first appeared as *Yb'sim* on Phoenician-Carthaginian coins. This became *Ebysos* to the Greeks, *Ebusus* to the Romans, and *Yebisah* to later Arab settlers. At the etymological root of the name is the deity Bes, a jolly, bearded dwarf whom the Phoenicians shared with the ancient Egyptians. The plump little fellow — whose music drowned out the rage of the angry spirits — was a natural for Ibiza's modern disco destiny.

In 654 B.C. the Carthaginian colonists built the hilltop acropolis of Ereso, which was to become today's Ibiza Town. From their strongholds in North Africa and at Cadiz on the Spanish mainland, they challenged the Roman Empire for domination of the Mediterranean region. Ibiza's contribution to the Carthaginians' war effort came from its lead mines (active until the 20th century), which provided ammunition for the great general Hannibal in his epic battles with the Romans. The colonists' commercial interest in Ibiza lay also in its vast, still-productive salt flats. The salt was used to cure fish, which was exported (along with a much appreciated local fish sauce) to Carthage, back to Tyre and Sidon, and later to neighboring Majorca and Menorca. Ibiza also made a tidy profit from its exports of wool and dyes for textiles.

The Romans

The Romans never really infiltrated Ibiza. Even after they defeated the Carthaginian general Hannibal in 202 B.C., the

Gods and Goddesses

Ibiza's gods have always been a lusty lot. Originating in the eastern Mediterranean, the deities revered by the Carthaginians were imbued with a sensuality that has remained the island's trademark. Surviving busts of the chief goddess, Tanit, who was worshipped for her fertility, portray her with thick lips and luxuriant hair styles. She was the consort of Baal Hammon, king of Carthaginian gods, whom the Romans identified with Saturn. The riotous festivities that took place in his name during what is now the Christmas season are now a year-round phenomenon on modern Ibiza.

Many clay figurines have been found in ancient pottery recently unearthed near the Puig des Molins necropolis below Ibiza Town's Dalt Vila. Most popular of these was the dwarf god, Bes. This outrageous fellow was often portrayed with goggle eyes, protruding tongue, bowlegs, bushy tail, and even a crown of feathers. He, too, has his modern counterpart in the island's nightlife.

Life and Art in the Carthaginian Colony

Believing that Ibiza's clay could repel animals and harmful substances, the Carthaginians considered it a holy island. From the time of its colonization by the North African nation, Ibiza grew steadily in importance, and for centuries it ranked as one of the major commercial and military centers in the Mediterranean. Decline set in with the defeat of Carthage by the Romans (146 B.C.), yet Ibiza held fast to the fierce gods and sometimes gruesome customs of the past, preserving the Phoenician traditions of Carthage long into the Roman period.

Archaeologists paint a fascinating picture of life, death, and ritual in the Carthaginian colony. More than 20 ancient sites have been explored over the past century, and a wealth of objects has come to light. The most important necropolis (burial site) is at Puig des Molins, where there are some 4,000 tombs, though fewer than 300 have actually been uncovered. Here you can see the spacious burial chambers constructed for rich citizens of the capital, who were laid to rest in enormous stone sarcophagi surrounded by the paraphernalia of a happy afterlife: unguent jars, lanterns, terracotta statuettes of deities, and ostrich eggs decorated with symbols of life and resurrection. The less affluent made do with a shallow tomb or simple sarcophagus set into the hillside. Cheaper still — if less roomy — was an ordinary vase just large enough to hold the ashes of the departed.

Other important Carthaginian sites include the sanctuaries of Isla Plana, a little peninsula jutting into the Bahía d'Ibiza, and Es Cuieram, a cave near Sant Vicent in the sparsely populated northeastern quadrant of the island. From the earliest period of Carthaginian colonization, Isla Plana was a holy place. People came here to seek protection, especially from difficulties in childbirth and from childhood illnesses. Es Cuieram was dedicated to the cult of the goddess Tanit, which reached its peak from the fourth to the second centuries B.C. The isolation of the cave did not stop believers from depositing gold medallions and hundreds of terracotta figures here. Nearly all the terracottas were blackened by fire. Together with the quantities of bones and ashes uncovered in the cave, this suggests some kind of funerary rite at Es Cuieram.

For all its vitality, the island's Carthaginian culture died out. By the close of the Roman era, Es Cuieram, Isla Plana, Puig des Molins, and Ibiza's other sanctuaries and necropolises lay abandoned and forgotten. Then, after the Arab conquests in the ninth and tenth centuries A.D., thieves plundered the tombs of Puig des Molins, stripping them of precious gold jewelry. However, the thieves added something of their own to the archaeological record by leaving behind the lamps that illuminated their search.

Sadly, the plunder continued into the 20th century, with unscrupulous archaeologists amassing private collections of Carthaginian art and artifacts in the course of "official" excavations. There were plenty of clandestine digs, too. One antiques dealer from Mallorca kept a legion of islanders on the lookout for additions to his collection. He later exhibited the finds in Barcelona and pocketed the proceeds. Not long after, Barcelona's archaeological museum acquired every last object for a handsome sum.

Although many key pieces of Carthaginian art have been dispersed or lost, many more are on display in Ibiza's archaeological museums. Gold work, jewelry, the painted spheres of ostrich eggs, and exquisitely modeled terracottas all provide rare but valuable insight into the island's past. These ritual and ornamental objects perplex and intrigue. Even in their paucity, they do at least offer a tantalizing glimpse of the spirit of Carthage which Rome had been so determined to destroy.

Romans' influence was restrained. Only with the fall of Carthage in 146 B.C. did they manage to make inroads. However — as local historians proudly emphasize — Ibiza was neither conquered nor annexed by Rome but, rather, confederated, retaining considerable autonomy. For centuries to come the old Carthaginian traditions were allowed to continue on Ibiza alongside the new Roman way of life.

On the other hand, the empire left a much more decisive imprint on the Iberian Peninsula, where language, culture, and government were all heavily influenced by Rome and where, in particular, the Romans' engineering genius was evident in the construction of roads, aqueducts, and monuments.

The Romans did exploit Ibiza's natural resources. They exported salt from the southern end of the island and lead

Tunnel to the past: through an old bulwark and into Dalt Vila. These splendid fortifications are several centuries old.

from the mines of Sant Carles, and they carried on the Phoenician technique of extracting a purple dye from shellfish, which was used for imperial cloaks. In addition, they found a moneymaker in the islanders' exotic aromatic sauce of decomposed fish innards. Called *garum*, it was considered a great delicacy by Romans and Greeks alike. Today it is but a historical footnote; local cooks use nothing more pungent than garlic.

The Arabs

After prolonged peace and productivity, the year A.D. 426 launched an era of strife and violence. Ibiza, along with the rest of what is now Spain, was invaded and sacked by the Germanic tribe of Vandals. Centuries of foreign rule followed, with the Vandals succeeded first by the Byzantines and then by Arab forces attacking Ibiza in 711.

Rebounding from initial defeats by the Carolingian forces of the Franks, the Arabs completed their conquest of the Balearic Islands by 903. They alternated sporadic violent forays of piracy on the high seas with equally energetic development of the islands' economy and agriculture. The Arabs' ingenious network of irrigation ditches is still in operation on Ibiza. Most enduring of their legacies is the pure North African design of their houses, justly admired by the great Swiss architect Le Corbusier: simple combinations of dazzling white round-cornered cubes, thick walled to keep cool in summer and warm in winter.

Apart from a few ceramics in the museum, the artistic achievements of the Arabs survives best in the island's haunting folk music. Otherwise, the Arab heritage crops up in a few local place names, some words in the Ibicenco dialect, and — most vivid reminder of all — the dark, brooding eyes of so many islanders. (Spanish writers still refer to their

North African colonizers as "Moors," and Europeans use the term "Moorish" to refer to anything reflecting the pan-Arab culture of the medieval and Renaissance periods).

Christianity Comes to Ibiza

In the 12th century Ibiza was drawn into the ongoing fight between Islamic and Christian forces for control of the Mediterranean world. With the Crusaders' wars raging in Palestine and Syria, a Christian fleet arrived in Ibiza harbor on what was known as the "Crusade of Pisa" as part of a papal effort to break the Arabs' control on Spanish territory and to punish their brazen pirates.

Although this little local crusade of 1113 did not put an end to the Arab presence, it did herald the end of Islamic power

The Crusade of Pisa

The determination of Pope Paschal II in 1113 to make Ibiza safe for Christianity was not greeted by the islanders with the enthusiasm his Crusaders had been led to expect. The Crusade of Pisa, as it was called, arrived with a fleet of 500 warships to put an end to Islam's hold on the island as well as to the haven Ibiza provided for pirates. Instead of greeting the Christian forces as saviors, the Ibicencos rallied round the Arab viceroy, Abdul Manzor. They repelled one bloody charge after another and turned what the Crusaders had hoped would be a quick-fire invasion into a prolonged siege. In the end, however, people saw that the battle was lost and persuaded their leader to surrender. After dismantling what remained of the battered city walls, the Crusaders gave the islanders their first lesson in Christian piety by raping their women, forcing able-bodied men into service, and carrying off all the booty they could grab.

in Ibiza. Just over a century later, the wave of Christian victories over the Arabs on the Spanish mainland, known as the *Reconquista* (Reconquest) finally engulfed Ibiza. King James I of Aragon ordered the occupation of the islands under Catalonian forces commanded by Guillermo de Montgri, Bishop of Tarragona. After several bloody skirmishes, the troops launched a final pincer-movement assault on the Ibiza citadel. One flank of soldiers battered its way through the reinforced city walls. The other flank (so the popular legend goes) sneaked through a secret passage revealed to the invaders by the brother of the sheik himself. The legend claims the embittered traitor gave the game away because his passionate brother had seduced his wife.

Christianity holds firm in Ibiza since its arrival in the 12th century.

In this violent last act of August 1235, both Christianity and the Catalonian language came to Ibiza to stay. On the mainland, the Reconquest was practically completed by the earlier Christian victory at Navas de Tolosa in northern Andalusia in 1212 and the capture of Cordoba in 1236. However, it was only in 1492 that the Arabs were finally driven out of Granada, their last, brilliant stronghold on the peninsula.

An Era of Pirates

The year 1492 was crucial for Ibiza, and for Spain as a whole, for several reasons. On the mainland it marked the final defeat of the Arabs and — as one of Europe's more momentous forms of "ethnic cleansing" — the expulsion of Arabs and Jews from the newly united kingdom of Isabella and Ferdinand. In pursuit of the Spanish Inquisition, it was Isabella who expressed the goal of achieving *limpieza de sangre* ("blood cleansing").

It was also, of course, the year Christopher Columbus sailed to the Americas under the Spanish flag. For Ibiza, Spain's enrichment proved to be a catastrophe rather than a boon. The immense wealth of gold and silver brought back by the *conquistadores* diverted the attention of Spain away from the Mediterranean. Now the Spaniards were focused on the New World and on supremacy over their covetous northern European rivals. As a result, throughout the 16th and 17th centuries Ibiza sank into a stagnating backwater beset by plague (in 1662) and piracy.

The pirates came in large part from the Barbary Coast of North Africa. The fabled coast — embracing what are now Algeria and Tunisia — took its name from the region's ear-

Another "Pope"

One of the most villainous foreign swashbucklers sailing in Ibiza waters was a Spanish pirate from Gibraltar, Captain Miguel Novelli, alias "the Pope." Attacking the island from his cynically named ship, *Felicity,* he was confronted one day by Ibicenco captain Antonio Riquer midway between Ibiza and Formentera. Although Riquer had only eight guns compared to the Pope's dozen cannons, the local vessel won the day.

liest inhabitants, the Berbers. But the raiders of the 16th century were mainly Turks and Arabs who had been driven out of Spain. Most celebrated of the Turkish pirates was Barbarossa (Redbeard), who as Khayr Ad-Din became an admiral of the Ottoman imperial navy.

The Ibicencos fortified the bulwarks of Ibiza Town and built churches throughout the island as massive hilltop bastions against enemy incursions. A chain of sturdy, round stone watchtowers was constructed all along the island's coast. It is said that even the Ibicenco women's costume of several layers of petticoats was designed to protect them against pirates by simulating pregnancy.

In desperation, the islanders decided to meet fire with fire and formed their own bands of privateers. The local forces were subsequently "sponsored" by the French and British, who appreciated the islanders' skills in ship building. Suddenly, Barbarossa's pirates and others found their brigantines boarded on the open seas by fierce Ibicencos who commandeered their booty. Victory over the greatly feared "Pope" (see box, 20) was a much vaunted Ibizan triumph. Reflecting the morality of a period when piracy was regarded as merely an alternative form of commerce, Ibiza's port even raised a monumental obelisk to honor the exploits of its daring, home-grown buccaneers.

Political Turmoil

Ibiza had enjoyed (and still cherishes) a degree of autonomy, first from the kingdom of Aragon, then from Spain. The island forfeited a small measure of this autonomy in 1715 after supporting the Spanish branch of the Austrian Habsburg dynasty against the victorious Bourbons in the Spanish "Wars of Succession." Later, at the end of the 18th century, the independent-minded Ibicenco peasants resisted the Spanish government's effort to regroup them into parishes, preferring to remain scattered across the island. And by 1815 the Napoleonic Wars brought about an end to pirate raids in the region.

Ibiza thereafter continued to take a back seat as Spain slid into economic decline and political instability, losing its empire in the Americas and the Pacific by 1898. In the first third of the 20th century, neither military dictatorship under Primo de Rivera nor a constitutional monarchy under Alfonso XIII could guarantee domestic tranquility. The election victory by Republicans in 1931 drove the king into exile. Strikes, insurrection, and brutal military repression spread through the peninsula as the new republic was torn by bitter ideological divisions.

In February 1936 a Popular Front of socialists, communists, and anarchists came to power with the Republicans

Relic from the past. A mill wheel recalls more sedate times gone by in the now hot and happening resort of Sant Antoni.

against the fierce right-wing opposition of the fascist Falange Party supported by the church, the army, monarchists, and big business. Five months later, a military revolt led by General Francisco Franco in Spanish Morocco plunged the country into a three-year civil war that cost hundreds of thousands of lives.

Ibiza was the scene of two major episodes in the Spanish Civil War. Like neighboring Majorca, Ibiza yielded to its anti-Republican garrison at the outbreak of war in July 1936. Among the Balearic Islands, only Menorca resisted the first military rebellion. Then Republican forces chose Ibiza as the bridgehead for a counterattack. On 9 August a joint Catalan-Valencian force under Captain Alberto Bayo arrived in Ibiza's harbor with four transport ships escorted by a battleship, two destroyers, a submarine, and six aircraft. Ibicenco workers seized the 50-strong pro-Franco garrison. A subsequent assault on Majorca failed, but Ibiza (and Formentera) reverted to Republican control.

On 29 May 1937 another local incident nearly transformed the Spanish war into the world war for which it already seemed a rehearsal. The German battleship *Deutschland* lay at anchor off Ibiza when two Republican aircraft dropped bombs that killed 31 and wounded 74 other German sailors. Hitler ordered an immediate punitive attack, shelling the Andalusian town of Almería. The Spanish Republicans decided only reluctantly not to bomb the German fleet in the Mediterranean to bring other great powers into the war.

Modern Times

Franco's Spain stayed neutral throughout World War II but could not repair its own shattered economy. Even after 1945, reconstruction remained painfully slow. For Ibiza the breakthrough came with the introduction in the 1960s of wide-

Still standing — Old Ibiza makes for a fascinating glimpse back through history.

bodied jets and a significant surge in tourism. Following the expansion of the airport, the island entered the big league of international holiday resorts.

After the death of Franco in 1975, Juan Carlos I restored democracy to Spain, and moderates and democratic socialists emerged as the largest parties following the elections of 1977. In Ibiza the new freedoms meant the renaissance of Ibicenco language and culture after decades of suppression. The islands also began to participate in the affairs of the Catalonian region's newly won autonomy. Free speech and free elections were not the only innovations: gambling was legalized and nude bathing was sanctioned. Change swept through Ibiza dramatically, irrevocably, almost overnight.

Based largely on the tourist industry, the island's fortunes benefited considerably in 1986 when Spain joined what is now the European Union. In spite of high unemployment and the separatist rumblings of Catalans and Basques, the country's economic growth rate remained one of the highest in Europe throughout the last quarter of the 20th century. The wounds of Francoism were sufficiently healed for a right-wing prime minister, José María Aznar, to defeat socialist Felipe Gonzalez in 1996 without anyone fearing for democracy. Ibiza kept smiling.

Historical Landmarks

ca. 1600 B.C.	Earliest inhabitants build megalithic monuments.
654 B.C.	Carthaginians colonize Ibiza.
218–201 B.C.	Ibiza ammunition used in Carthage's war against Rome.
123 B.C.	Ibiza added to Roman confederation.
A.D. 426	Ibiza raided and sacked by Vandals.
903	Arab conquest of Balearic Islands complete.
1235	Christian rulers bring Reconquest to Ibiza.
1469	Marriage of Ferdinand II to Isabella unites Spain; Balearics become key Spanish posts in Mediterranean.
1492	Arabs and Jews expelled from Spain; Christopher Columbus sails to the Americas.
1500	Spain's transatlantic preoccupations send Balearics into decline; Barbary Coast piracy begins.
1662	Ibiza population decimated by plague.
1799–1815	Napoleonic Wars end pirate raids from North Africa.
1936	Left-wing Republican government opposed by General Franco and fascist Falange Party.
1936–39	Spanish Civil War: Ibiza captured by Republican forces.
1960s	Ibiza inundated by mass tourism with introduction of wide-bodied jets.
1975	Death of Franco, restoration of constitutional monarchy.
1981	King Juan Carlos I thwarts a military coup.
1986	Spain admitted to what is now European Union.
1996	Conservative José María Aznar replaces socialist Felipe Gonzalez as Spanish prime minister.

WHERE TO GO

Some visitors to the islands decide simply to stay put and enjoy the sun and water. They wander from hotel to beach and back again. Others will want to explore the island of Ibiza, starting with its three main urban centers: Ibiza Town, Sant Antoni, and Santa Eulària. But don't forget the classically Mediterranean landscape of the interior of the island, dotted with handsome white Ibicenco farmhouses. Concluding our tour of Ibiza is a driving tour of its magical rugged coastline.

An excursion out to the quieter little world of Formentera reveals a different landscape and scene: a desert island that is more relaxed, more rural, and thus more traditional. The beaches here are less crowded, and the overall atmosphere is laidback and lazy. Nevertheless, Formentera has resorts, hotels, restaurants, and nightclubs to satisfy those needing a few reminders of the high life.

IBIZA

Morning, noon, and night there is a feast for the senses everywhere you look on Ibiza — and you are often tempted to look everywhere at once. At breakfast time near the harbor in any of the major resorts, there is plenty of activity as the fishing boats come in or the elegant yachts prepare to go out. And the coffee in the portside café tastes just fine. Midmorning in Ibiza Town you might want to explore the boutiques of the Sa Penya quarter or walk up through the old Dalt Vila citadel to explore the fascinating Phoenician past in the museum or the rich Spanish Catholic culture in the cathedral.

After strolling up to the hilltop church in Santa Eulària for a view over the bay, you might develop an appetite, which you can satisfy at a variety of excellent restaurants. Then spend a lazy or active afternoon (depending on your inclination) in the sun, sea, and sand at any one of 56 beaches stretching around the island (see page 41).

Nature lovers will want to explore the many beautiful trails in the interior to take in the fragrances and colors of the wildflowers (see page 58). On the way, enjoy a little bird-watching along the cliffs or on the salt flats of Las Salinas (see page 48). Among your other options is a boat cruise to explore the coastline and discover otherwise inaccessible secluded coves for private swimming and diving. Or you can make a full day's outing to the island of Formentera. That leaves the evening for quiet dining or boisterous partying — or both — in the cool and hot spots in and around Sant Antoni and the other major resorts.

The island is divided administratively into five communes (districts): Ibiza Town, Sant Antoni, Santa Eulària, Sant Josep, and Sant Joan, each named after its principal urban center. Our tour visits each of the communes as we explore the towns, resorts, villages, hills, and coastline of Ibiza.

Wildflowers scattered across the hills show that Ibiza's countryside offers even more color than its nightclubs.

Ibiza Town (Eivissa)

The major focus of activity on the island is naturally enough its capital, **Ibiza Town (Eivissa)**, which is divided into four areas. Towering over it all is the old walled city, Dalt Vila ("higher town"). Between the ramparts and the port, La Marina is the main harbor district, packed with shops, bars, cafés, and restaurants. More modest is Sa Penya, a former fishing neighborhood extending east along the harbor's promontory. The modern district of Eixample (Castilian: Ensanche) stretches west and north from the town's main boulevard, Passeig de Vara de Rey.

Most visitors guiding themselves through a sightseeing day in Ibiza Town arrive by bus from one of the outlying resorts. The buses stop on Avinguda Isidoro Macabich, either at the station or opposite the Delegación del Gobierno building.

Nothing sleepy about this port — Ibiza Town's harbor is a constant spectacle of arrivals and departures.

Follow Isidoro Macabich east to the major intersection at Avinguda Ignacio Wallis. Turn right and a few hundred meters later you'll come to **Passeig Vara de Rey**, the town's attractive tree-lined esplanade, which some locals still call by its old name, S'Alamera (The Boulevard). As in most Spanish towns, here is where young and old alike gather in the early evening for the time-honored promenade (Spanish: *paseo;* Ibicenco: *passeig).* It owes its present name to one of the island's great heroes, General Joaquín Vara de Rey, commemorated here by a grand, rousing statue surrounded on its pedestal by bronze wreaths and allegorical figures. It was erected six years after the general died defending the colony of Cuba in the Spanish-American War of 1898.

A news agent here sells a wide selection of European publications. Pick up your favorite paper and take it to one of several outdoor cafés where a *café con leche* can last through a whole morning of basking in the sun, postcard writing, map reading, or watching the crowds. The cafés situated nearest to the port attract the chic and sophisticated, among others, who sit at tables covered with yellow tablecloths and are served by waiters dressed — with exaggerated formality by local standards — in smart bow ties and white jackets. Here also is where the town tycoons transact business in the civilized Spanish way: over sherry or brandy.

La Marina and Sa Penya

Now it's time for an unpackaged tour of the town. The most logical place to start is down at the harbor, around the corner from Vara de Rey. An imposing pier in the center of the dock area serves the liners from Palma, Barcelona, Valencia, and other scheduled ferry points. The passenger terminal is a modern building with a restaurant on top. From there or from the quayside there is plenty of activity to see as the gleam-

Island Highlights

Ibiza

Ibiza Town: the harbor, La Marina, and the atmospheric old-world streets of Sa Penya; when it all gets too much, relax at a waterside café.

Dalt Vila: the old walled town, now part of Ibiza Town, with sturdy defenses, cathedral, and museums.

Museo Monographic Puig des Molins: the one museum that should not be missed, it gives the best view of Ibiza's Phoenician beginnings.

Sant Antoni: once a fishing village, now a resort with a yacht-filled bay, fishing and ferry boats, and good beaches.

Coniera: the now-uninhabited island where General Hannibal is said to have been born; good for escaping the crowds and for walks among wildflowers and lizards.

Santa Eulària: former market center and the island's first town to attract foreign visitors, now boasting a fine selection of restaurants.

Sa Talaia: also known as Atalaya, at 475 m (1,560 ft) the highest point on the island; a challenging drive and/or hike with magnificent views.

Es Cuieram: secluded cave used as a Carthaginian burial ground; treasures uncovered here now on view in the archaeological museum in Dalt Vila.

Las Salinas: large salt flats found on both Ibiza and Formentera.

Formentera

Far de la Mola: 19th-century lighthouse featured in Jules Verne's Journey Round the Solar System, occupying a splendid position with wonderful views of Formentera.

Ca Na Costa: prehistoric stone circle dating from about 1600 B.C., still being excavated but open for viewing.

ing white ships load and unload their cargo and passengers. In front of the terminal, a traffic circle now surrounds the **Corsair Obelisk** (Obelisco a los Corsarios), perhaps the world's only monument in praise of privateers.

The district of **La Marina**, extending inland from the Obelisk to the old city walls, combines the traditional image of a Mediterranean port with all the modern amenities of a bustling tourist quarter. One white church is dedicated to the quarter's patron saint, known variously as Sant Elm or San Salvador. Beyond the church in the direction of the old walled city is the Mercat de ses Verdures (fruit and vegetable market). In the narrow streets, classical Ibicenco houses — white cubic forms, many leaning at an angle, their black wrought-iron balconies decked out with a few flowers — have been transformed into fashion boutiques and souvenir shops, their goods cascading onto the sidewalks. More color is added by tourists' gaudy holiday clothes, while the whole scene is observed from bars and cafés by sleepy night owls shading their eyes against the bright sun.

In the neighborhood named after the harbor promontory, **Sa Penya** (The Rock), the streets are even narrower and noticeably poorer. Tourist cafés and restaurants are largely confined to the waterfront. At night this district is a popular entertainment area. By day, as the streets climb toward Dalt Vila, a few fishermen can still be seen making their way home, passing their black-clad wives laden with shopping. Passersby should watch out for the drip of laundry drying on upper floors and for scampering children or loping dogs and cats. Wafting out of the windows are the aromas of coffee, spices, fish, and baking bread. The octagonal Mercat de Peix (fish market) is close to the ramparts of the old city.

Dalt Vila

Opposite the fruit and vegetable market is the main entrance to the old walled citadel, **Dalt Vila** (there are two other ancient gateways through the walls). A ceremonial ramp leads across what used to be a moat into an impressive gateway, the **Portal de ses Taules**. Over the arch is a Latin inscription dating the wall to 1585, during the reign of Philip II of Spain. Standing on either side are gracefully robed, headless white marble statues. They were unearthed on the spot during a 16th-century construction project. According to the barely decipherable Latin inscriptions, one of the statues honors a Roman senator; the other is a tribute from an aristocratic Roman family to Juno, the Roman goddess.

Historians believe the Carthaginians initially constructed a wall here — with foundations shared by the current city walls — although there are no remains of it. The Arabs built a second wall, of which towers and remnants are evident today. Ibiza's seven bulwark defenses are almost completely intact. The present bulwarks date back to 1554, when Emperor Charles V ordered reconstruction of the wall, whose thickness was 3.5 m (11.5 ft). The fortifications, which are among the best preserved in Europe, have been declared a national monument. They still completely encircle the old citadel and remain an admirable testimony to the military technology of the Renaissance.

The tunnel through the great wall at Portal de ses Taules leads to a classic quadrangle planned for royal parades, the **Patio de Armas** (Arsenal Square). Today, the pomp under the porticos has been replaced by artisans peddling their jewelry and leatherwork, often original and inexpensive. The square, which also houses the Contemporary Arts Museum, leads into the first of several wide, open plazas linked by a maze of narrow alleys climbing the citadel hill.

A map isn't really necessary in Dalt Vila, an old town of steep cobbled streets, curious dead ends, and unexpected vistas. The most important directions are simply up and down: "up" leads eventually to the hilltop cathedral and fortress, and "down" inevitably leads to one of three gates through the wall to the new town. The variations are almost infinite, and this is one time when wrong turns can actually be recommended. Every zigzag is likely to bring another delight — a sweep of bougainvillea, a baroque doorway, a fashionable restaurant, or a new perspective on the sea and city below.

Portal to the past — the main entrance to Dalt Vila, Portal de ses Taules.

When you reach an impressive plaza with a 16th-century church and whitewashed town hall, you might feel you've come to the top of the town. But you haven't. Catch your breath here and admire the view down the cliffside from the edge of the city wall before continuing to ascend the narrow streets.

At last you reach the uppermost cobbled square. The **Cathedral of Santa Maria de las Neus**, on your right, was built in the 13th century on the site of a Roman temple and an Islamic mosque. It was subsequently renovated in the 16th and 18th centuries. The resulting architectural eccentricities on the outside are matched in interest by a number of medieval works of art inside. More works can be seen in the museum attached to the cathedral. If you wonder why, in this sunny climate, the church is dedicated to "Our Lady of the Snows," it is because the Catalans chose the patron saint whose feast day, 5 August, came closest to the date of their final victory here (three days later) over the Arabs.

Across the square is the **Museo Arqueològic de Dalt Vila** (Archaeological Museum), which houses one of Ibiza's two collections of Phoenician and Roman antiquities (together constituting one of the world's great treasuries of Carthaginian art). All the relics on display were discovered on the island; they range from statues and urns to priceless jewelry and coins. The museum occupies part of what was once the town's university. Luckily, many of the items are self-explanatory, which is fortunate because most descriptions are printed in Spanish only. Keep in mind the manner of writing dates: *III siglo a. J.C.* means third century B.C. and *XII siglo d. J.C.* means 12th century A.D. The museum is compact enough to be covered in half an hour or so.

When visiting churches, you should not wear shorts, tank tops, or backless dresses.

Puig des Molins

Making your way over to Portal Nou, another gateway through the great wall, you'll find yourself in the modern part of town amid offices, luxury apartments, and shops. Four streets away is the **Museo Monografic Puig des Molins**, a modern, spacious new town museum. The museum is built on the edge of a particularly attractive hill, which is covered with olive trees and wildflowers and is known as **Puig des Molins** (Hill of the Windmills). Here the Carthaginians, and later the Romans, buried their dead with respectful ritual. The artifacts displayed in the museum were

Museums and Galleries

Note: All listed museums are in Ibiza Town.

Museo Arqueològic de Dalt Vila (at the top of the old walled town). Exhibits from all over the island, especially Carthaginian terra cottas and fertility figures from sanctuaries and necropolises, plus a selection of Roman and Arabic artifacts. Open 10am–1pm and 4pm–7 pm; closed Sunday afternoon and Monday. Free admission.

Museo Monografic Puig des Molins (Via Romana). On display are articles discovered in the Carthaginian necropolis nearby, including scarabs, unguent jars, jewelry, mirrors, and razors. Superb collection of terra cottas. Be sure to take a look at the powerful series of goddesses, imperial in their elaborate necklaces, gold nose rings, and earrings. Visit the necropolis itself, where several burial chambers are open to view. The museum is open daily in summer 5pm–8pm and in winter 4pm–7pm. Admission: 300 pesetas.

Museo Catedral (adjacent to Ibiza's cathedral, at the summit of the old town). Contains municipal and church memorabilia. Featured item is a monstrance (receptacle for the host) from Majorca, a prized example of medieval silverware dating from the late-15th century. Open daily in summer 10am–1pm and, in winter, on Tuesday and Friday 10am–1pm. Admission: 100 pesetas.

Museo Arte Contemporáneo (Arsenal Square, alongside the city wall just inside the old town). Modern art, one-man shows, and group exhibitions in a venerable setting. Open Monday through Friday 10am–2pm and 5pm–7pm; Saturday 10am–1:30pm. Admission: 200 pesetas.

Art galleries. These are in Ibiza Town and on the road to Sant Josep and Sant Miquel, as well as in Sant Antoni and Santa Eulària. Special shows are advertised. The island attracts artists of all styles and levels of expertise, and the sheer volume of their output is prodigious. Ibiza's artists also display their works in many tourist hotels and expatriate bars.

all unearthed on the spot; again, the inscriptions are in Spanish only. Outstanding is a terracotta bust of the Carthaginian goddess Tanit.

Outside and around the corner of the building you'll find a cave-like entrance to the funerary site itself, where several burial chambers have been cleared and illuminated. There are some 4,000 vaults in all. After you've seen the museum's works of art — which were buried next to the bodies — the crypt shouldn't seem too gloomy a sight. If you feel a little claustrophobic, then wander to the far side of the hill for a view of the sea and, on the proverbial clear day, Formentera. Nearby is the beach of Figueretes ("little fig trees"), a popular place for bathing.

☛ Sant Antoni

From Ibiza Town, a short drive to the west coast of the island brings you to **Sant Antoni.** In the past 30 years Sant Antoni has transformed itself from a pretty, low-key little fishing port into a large-scale, exuberant, planned tourist resort expanding its boundaries ever farther around and beyond the town's magnificent bay. Under the Romans, the grand sweep of the harbor earned the name "Portus Magnus," which survives today in the town's complete name, Sant Antoni de Portmany.

Romantics might regret that the few remaining fishing boats have to make their way around every manner of sailing boat from sleek yachts to powerful motor launches, passing glass-bottom boats, big ferries, and even bigger freighters. The municipality itself rubs its hands at the newly found prosperity of mass tourism, with gleaming white high-rise hotels whose apparently tireless guests satisfy their lust for life in some of the island's most boisterous bars and discos.

With Sant Antoni's local population close to 15,000, the ongoing expansion has its pros and cons. The newer hotels have been built on out-of-town beaches, providing doorstep swimming and sunbathing but requiring a ride to shopping and nightlife. Conversely, those staying in town sometimes have to travel to find a desirable beach. To compensate, buses do seem to go everywhere, and there are ferry connections as well. Part of the Sant Antoni adventure is planning each day's outing with local maps and bus timetables. The west coast of Ibiza has a terrific choice of first-rate beaches — all an easy day-trip from Sant Antoni — for family bathers, windsurfers, or hot-shot scuba divers.

The town itself has managed to preserve a few of its old stucco houses among the brash new buildings. In the past, the heart of town was located four streets up the hill from the seafront. From its elevated position overlooking the bay, the sturdy white 14th-century **Church of Sant Antoni**, replaced an Islamic mosque and served as a fortress with watchtower to warn against assaults by pirates and other invaders. Its formidable appearance is softened by an attractive patio surrounded by graceful arches.

Along the waterfront, the center of activity is the **Passeig Marítim** (Maritime Promenade), a bay-front park

The Church of Sant Antoni has also served as a fortress with a watchtower.

area reclaimed from the sea and now covered with trees, flowers, a fountain, benches, and a proliferation of outdoor cafés and restaurants.

The small ferryboats (mostly converted fishing vessels) operate to beaches near and far; usually, but not necessarily, the beaches farther from town are better. All beaches served by public transportation have snack bars, beach chairs for hire, parasols, and other amenities. Note that lifeguards are a rare exception on Ibiza, with practically none at all on duty on a regular all-day basis. This is not *Baywatch.*

The municipal bus station is right next to the bay-front Promenade. Buses to the beaches are cheaper and faster than ferries, if less adventurous. However, bus service is restricted to beaches close to Sant Antoni. The island's rugged topography and municipal politics have so far prevented a highway going all the way around the coast. Many of the best beaches can therefore be reached only on bumpy, dusty trails more suitable for mules than buses.

Signs:
Llegadas "Arrivals"
Salidas "Departures"

Dominating the mouth of Sant Antoni Bay is the gaunt silhouette of the island of **Coniera** (or "Conejera"; the names mean "rabbit's warren" or "burrow"). According to legend, this uninhabited island was the birthplace of the great Carthaginian warrior Hannibal. Its other claim to fame is an automatic lighthouse with a signal visible at distances up to 48 km (30 miles). From Sant Antoni, Coniera appears to be almost hopelessly inhospitable, but a tiny, hidden harbor makes it possible for boats to moor here. The island is well covered with tenacious pines, a delightful variety of wildflowers, and crowds of friendly lizards. The swimming is, however, unsuitable for children, and the tender-footed should beware of the sea urchins' spiny quills.

An excursion 2 km (just over a mile) north from Sant Antoni leads to the early Christian subterranean chapel of **Santa Inés**, built complete with nave and chancel inside a natural cave. Excavations here in 1907 uncovered artifacts from Carthaginian, Roman, and Arab eras. The cave is open to the public Monday 9am–noon and Saturday 7pm–9pm.

In Santa Eulària's fine church, admire the elaborate Baroque design of the altar.

Santa Eulària

On the south coast — east of Ibiza Town — is the island's second-largest town, **Santa Eulària** (population 19,500). It has grown into a prosperous resort with a pleasant, lighthearted atmosphere that seems deliberately less frenetic than its rival at Sant Antoni. Foreign artists and writers made their home here long before commercial tourism arrived and can justly claim credit for the town's enduring reputation for good restaurants and bars.

The only river on Ibiza, with its source barely 12 km (7.5 miles) to the north near Santa Gertrudis, gives the town its formal name: Santa Eulària del Riu. In the past, the river was skillfully used by the Arabs for irrigation, establishing the town's role as an agricultural center. Although ever-increasing water consumption has reduced the river to little more than a trickle today, Santa Eulària (Castilian: Santa Eulalia) is still surrounded by fruit and vegetable gardens, green pine forests, and extensive farmlands to the north. Its commune (administrative district) comprises the towns of Santa Gertrudis, Sant Carles, and Jesus and stretches along the island's southeast coast from Cap Martinet, near Talamanca, almost all the way north to Cala Sant Vicent.

History has divided the town into two distinct areas: the old inland community nestled around the church on **Puig de Missa** hill and the modern town that has extended in more peaceful times down to the port. Atop Puig de Missa, the dazzling white **Church of Santa Eulària** is worth a visit both for its historic interest and for its magnificent view over the bay. The core of the fortress church was built in 1568 by Italian architect Giovanni Battista Calvi, who followed up his ramparts for Ibiza Town with a similarly sturdy defensive tower here. Chapels on each side of the presbytery were added in the 17th century to complete the cruciform floorplan.

One of the island's characteristic cubic white houses here has been transformed into a small folklore museum, the **Museo Etnogràfic**. Among the many delightful flower gardens on Puig de Missa there is a particularly cheerful one in the church cemetery. The little hill also offers a view of the river and its two bridges, one modern and one old and cobbled, possibly Roman in origin.

In the modern district of **Sa Vila Nova**, the arcaded town hall (Ajuntament) looks out across a plaza down a broad esplanade to the seafront. A monument on the plaza commemorates a shipwreck of 1913. Having shed its name of Passeig Generalissimo Franco, the tree-lined esplanade is now popularly known as "La Rambla" in almost self-mocking architectural homage to Barcelona's celebrated thoroughfare. On the seafront promenade, Passeig Marítim, people stroll past the cafés and shops along the splendid sweep of Santa Eulària bay from the yachting harbor west to the mouth of the river.

Island Beaches

Ibiza

Cala Comte: panoramic sandy and rocky beach; suitable for both snorkelers and children.

Cala Llonga: a shallow bay surrounded by pine groves; fine white sand, good for young children; restaurants, sunbeds, pedalos, windsurfing.

Cala Tárida: white sand and flat rocks, an activity-oriented beach with plenty of water sports; restaurant and beach bar.

Cala Vedella: popular but often busy family beach, with fine white sand flanked by rocks; lots of amenities including bars, pedalos, windsurfing.

Es Canar: popular sandy beach and cove with fine sands and a backdrop of pinewoods; favorite for water sports but safe for children, too.

Playa Cavallet: the island's official nudist beach (but good for birdwatching, too), with fine white sand plus rocks at southern end; complete with amenities but little shade.

Playa d'en Bossa: known as the island's longest beach (2.5 km/1.5 miles), close to Ibiza Town and very busy; popular especially for its lively beach bar; pedalos and schools for diving and motorboating.

Formentera

Cala Sahona: attractive sandy beach, the most popular on Formentera and often busy.

Platja de Mitjorn: stretching around a wide bay, a pebbly beach that is Formentera's longest (8 km/5 miles).

Playa Es Pujols: for many, the best beach on the island, despite the nearby modern construction; good sands, shallow water, and lots of amenities.

The Island's Interior

The main road linking Ibiza Town with Sant Antoni passes through the farming village of Sant Rafel. The 18th-century church is notable for its façade and belfry, with baroque curves that are a rarity on Ibiza. The little plaza in front offers a fine view back down over groves of orange, almond, and fig trees to the distant skyline of Ibiza Town. However, Sant Rafel's most celebrated "monument" is in fact the island's most notorious disco, the extravagant Privilege (just southeast of town), so beware of the late-night traffic on this already busy highway. Of course, if you can't beat 'em, join 'em. In the more tranquil daylight hours, visit the local pottery workshops.

A smaller road farther to the west also links Sant Antoni to Ibiza Town. From it, a signposted turnoff just west of Sant Josep takes you along paved and then bumpy dirt roads to the island's highest point, **Sa Talaia**, 475 m (1,560 ft) above sea level. Its name, meaning "the watchtower," is amply justified by the grand view over the southern half of the island and, on a clear day, west to the Spanish mainland — and by the remains of an old fortress at the top.

The village of **Sant Josep** is capital of the island's largest commune, covering all of southern Ibiza from the bay of Sant Antoni east to Playa d'en Bossa. In an enchanting setting of juniper, fig, carob, and pine trees, Sant Josep proudly maintains local customs and is well known for its craftwork. Several shops sell local embroidery and other hand-crafted souvenirs. Embellishing the immaculate, traditional white cubic houses, flower gardens are given the same meticulous care. The town regularly shows its attachment to the region's folklore with col-

Fuel:
***sin plomo* ("unleaded")**
***gasolina* ("regular")**
***super* ("premium")**
***gas-oil* ("diesel")**

orful festivals of dancing in the forecourt of its 18th-century church. The music strikingly combines the rhythms of Arabic music with songs of the Christian era. The bell-towered church — like that of Sant Antoni — was damaged by fire at the outbreak of the Spanish Civil War. The baroque altarpiece was completely destroyed but has been replaced by a faithful replica. The handsome original wooden rosary pulpit, created in 1763 by José Sànchez Ocaña, is intact.

Pretty, rustic earthenware pottery in Sant Josep, a town renowned for its crafts.

Just south of the Sant Josep–Ibiza Town road, the illuminated stalactites and stalagmites of the privately owned **Cova Santa** (Holy Cave) make it a popular attraction (open 9am–1:30pm). The name is thought to derive from its role as a sanctuary — 25 m (82 ft) deep — for people fleeing pirate attacks from the 16th to 18th centuries.

Located a short drive northeast from Ibiza Town, the village of **Jesus** boasts in its 15th-century **Church of Nuestra Señora** one of the island's most important artistic treasures. A transitional work incorporating late Gothic and Italian Renaissance influences, the admirable triptych altarpiece (dated ca. 1498) is attributed to the Valencian workshop of Rodrigo de Osona. It stands in the Gothic-vaulted presbytery and is usually accessible to the public only on Thursday mornings, but group visits at other times can be arranged through the Ibiza Town tourist office.

A few miles southwest of Ibiza Town on the way to the island airport, is the charming little village of **Sant Jordi**. Here you will see one of the most remarkable of all the island's many churches that have had to serve as both house of worship and fortress to defend the community. This church

Spirits and Whitewash

Some country folk in the island's interior still practice elements of pre-Christian pagan beliefs and rituals. In many Ibicenco hamlets, old women credited with supernatural powers treat ailing people and animals. These spiritual healers use incantations and herbal medicines.

According to tradition, certain bottles contain little devils or imps *(diablillos)*. If a housewife opens the bottle without following the proper procedure, she is plagued by all manner of minor domestic problems. That, at least, is the story she tells her irate husband.

Every springtime the hardy women of Ibiza set out with almost religious enthusiasm to whitewash their houses. Some anthropologists believe that the whitewash craze might be derived from some remote Phoenician ritual. Local poet Fajarnes Cardona called it "that whiteness, an exorcism of all that's sordid."

Architects point out that each house represents a conjunction of modular one-room units, infinitely expandable to suit conditions. Instead of the traditional Spanish patio, Ibiza has opted for open verandas with stately arches. Triangular-topped chimneys, outside staircases, and the rounded cubic shapes (probably inherited centuries ago from North African settlers, Phoenician or Arab) have inspired modern architects from all over the world.

boasts the imposing battlements and solid rectangular form of a castle keep; there is only a little belfry with a cross on top to indicate that it is, in fact, a church. The largely 16th-century present edifice replaced a smaller medieval church. With the danger of pirate attacks receding, more graceful arched and domed side chapels were added in the 18th century.

On the northern side of the island, the 14th-century **Church of Sant Miquel** affords a hilltop view of the distant sea. In the interior, the chapel walls and vaults are decorated with frescoes that are mostly black and white. The churchyard has an interesting collection of artifacts from the village's past, including a wine press and grain mill. The spacious arcaded patio, dating from the 18th century, is now regularly used for festivities that feature vigorous Ibicenco dancing.

Other inland villages well worth exploring in the relatively uncrowded northern half of the island are **Santa Agnes**, up on its Corona plateau; **Sant Mateu**, beautifully set among almond, fig, and olive trees; **Sant Joan**, with its enchanting little church and cemetery surrounded by fragrant pine forests; and the livelier **Sant Carles**, famous for the Las Dalias "hippie market" of 1960s paraphernalia. When you visit these villages, take a look at the traditional houses, always simple in form and furniture. Notice also the built-in baking ovens, still in daily use. The country barns have ornate cobblestone and brick flooring.

Around the Coast

The easiest way to explore Ibiza's 170 km (105 miles) of coastline is obviously by boat. Nonetheless, drivers can reach many of the fine beaches and take in much of the glorious coastline with careful planning and map reading. But be aware that there is no continuous coastal road. You will often have to go far inland if you want to travel from one beach to another.

We'll start at the top of the compass and work clockwise around the island. The northernmost tourist center is **Portinatx** (pronounced "port-ee-NATCH"). To get there from the fertile farmland of the center of the island, you drive over substantial hills, alongside cliffs, and finally down to a surprisingly placid sea. The natural beauty of the area — sandy beaches, unusual rock formations, and picturesque groves of juniper and pine trees — has brought in much development that is not always quite so attractive.

Local historians point out that during Spanish naval maneuvers just off Ibiza in 1929, Alfonso XIII came ashore here. Immediately, the name of the place was officially changed to Portinatx del Rey. Perhaps from the international point of view, a more momentous event was the shooting of part of the film *South Pacific* on Portinatx beach.

A bit farther down the island's east coast, the splendid cove of **Cala de Sant Vicenç** is an increasingly successful resort center. While exceptionally hilly and circuitous, the road is

Haven fit for a king — Portinatx nestles between cliffs and is marked by unusual rock formations.

good enough to handle a stream of tourist buses, and the beach itself is likely to be crowded. Up in the hills behind Cala Sant Vicenç, after a rough hike over sometimes difficult terrain, you can visit a cave called **Es Cuieram**. Many archaeological treasures have been unearthed here on the grounds of an ancient temple dedicated to the Carthaginian goddess Tanit. Most of the artifacts can be viewed at the archaeological museums in Dalt Vila and Puig des Molins. In any case, the cave itself is a good place to seek temporary shelter from the midday sun.

Much of the coastline south from Sant Vicent is good sandy beach, very popular with visitors (tourists and locals alike) from Sant Carles. Areas served by roads have been built up and tend to be crowded at the height of summer. You have to wander farther afield — or come in by boat — to find more seclusion on the sand and a place for your beach towel.

Almost due east of Es Figueral is the offshore isle of **Tagomago**, now linked to the mainland of Ibiza by regular excursion boats. Although the beach at Tagomago is too narrow for sunbathing, the swimming is superb. It's worth the effort to ramble up to the extraordinary lighthouse at the top of the hill — past various abandoned farms amid fields of wildflowers — for the sweeping sea vistas you'll encounter along the way.

Es Canar has become a major tourist center that now sprawls along several beaches and includes abundant nightlife. There's yet another popular weekly "hippie market" in nearby **Punta Arabí**, to which special bus services and excursions run from Santa Eulària. It is also a pickpocket's paradise, so watch your belongings carefully.

Hikers will want to try the coastal path from Es Canar southwest to Santa Eulària and beyond. It winds its way past piney coves, mysterious cliffs, and quiet beaches. For some this might sound like hard work, but don't despair: beach-bar refreshment is never far away.

To the south of Santa Eulària, **Cala Llonga** is just what its name describes: a long cove that, from several vantage points, looks like a Norwegian fjord. Hotels and apartment construction push back into the hills, and locals as well as daytrippers from Santa Eulària throng the deep, sandy beach. But Cala Llonga's worst problems are fortunately a thing of the past, and the pollution that was once rampant has been halted by the construction of a sewage plant some distance away.

"Full tank, please!"
Llénelo, por favor!
(lyay-nay-lo por fah-bhor)

An impressive rocky coastline with a backdrop of verdant hills continues southward to **Talamanca**, a heavily developed beach with a fine view of Ibiza Town. On the other side of the capital is the hotel complex of **Figueretas**, and then the long, straight seafront beach of **Playa d'en Bossa**. This was once the scene of a famous "mis-"development plan: a 600-room luxury hotel had to be demolished just before opening for business — because it had mistakenly been built directly on the flight path to Ibiza's airport.

Near the salt flats at the southern tip of the island are some hard-to-reach, mostly unspoiled beaches. Among them is **Playa Cavallet**, which is officially reserved for nude bathing. Other nearby attractions include the port called **La Canal**, from which the salt is exported. The sprawling salt flats of ☛ **Las Salinas**, nearly 990 acres (400 hectares) at or just below sea level, have a fascination of their own. The white mountains of dry salt and the shimmering patterns on the heavy water remind some people of the Dead Sea: a desert outpost in an otherwise green and hospitable land. Providing the mainstay of the economy for this area, some 60,000 tons (54,400 metric tons) of salt a year are harvested here.

More sand or rock beaches continue north and west from the salt flats, but they become less and less accessible. The scenery is more spectacular where the hamlet of **Es Cubells** (reached by road from Sant Josep) occupies a land's-end

Wildlife Watch

Ibiza claims a unique zoological attraction. The celebrated Ibicenco hound is as skinny — and fast — as a greyhound but has a coat that is typically red with white markings. It has a long snout, alert big ears, and eyes as mysterious as a Siamese cat's. This hungry-looking dog (*podenco* to the islanders) has a history dating back thousands of years, perhaps to the dog portrayed on the walls of ancient Egyptian temples. It is said to be less intelligent than most common mongrels but was introduced to the US in the 1950s and exhibited at dog shows in the "miscellaneous class."

Strictly nocturnal, the little spotted or striped genet can be seen — very rarely — hunting its even smaller prey up in the mountain woods. In fact, there are no truly dangerous animals or poisonous insects and plants on Ibiza. The only reptiles are harmless lizards, of which there are two dozen varieties, usually found sunning themselves on rocks or foraging among pine cones. One species of lizard might be found in your hotel, possibly clinging to the ceiling. Remember: do not disturb. These fellows are useful allies — they catch mosquitoes.

Birdwatchers will enjoy classifying a variety of species that use the Balearics as a stopover during migration. The salt flats of both Ibiza and Formentera are good places to spot the wood-sandpiper (distinguished by its greenish-yellow legs), You can also find the raucous Old World bittern, tufted heron, black-winged stilt, Audouin seagull, Eleonore falcon, and bald buzzard. On rocky coastlines you might catch a rare glimpse of the black and white Manx shearwater (Puffinus puffinus, also known to Mediterraneans as the "Englishmen's puffin").

position overlooking rocks and the blue sea. A theological seminary is idyllically perched above the rocky crest.

A bit father up the island's southwest coast is **Cala d'Hort**, a small, isolated cove with clear water. Attractive enough in its own right, this peaceful little wilderness is enhanced by spectacular views of the isles of Es Vedrà and the smaller Es Vedranell, two rocky sentinels opposite the 18th-century Savinar watchtower. Just inland are the **Ses Països de Cala d'Hort**, excavated remains of a Carthaginian settlement dating back to the fifth century B.C. and later occupied by the Romans.

On the west coast leading up toward Sant Antoni Bay are some of the finest beaches on the island. Water sports enthusiasts dispute the merits of **Cala Bassa**, **Cala Vedella**, **Cala Tárida**, and **Cala Comte**, but each has something special to offer. At these coves you can enjoy clean, crystal-clear water and gently sloping white sandy beaches. There are good road connections between Sant Antoni and both Cala Tárida and Cala Vedella, with the result that both bays have now been developed. You can also reach Cala Bassa and Cala Comte by road (with good bus service) or by boat. The combination of red and grayish rocks, white sands, green pines, and deep blue sky and sea is striking. Local kids love exploring the nearby caves.

Past the small coves north of Sant Antoni, the rest of the coastal circle is something of a "no man's land" of choppy seas and razor-sharp rocks. Only one real road leads to the coast in this whole quadrant. The beach of **Port de Sant Miquel**, which once had the Arabic name of Balansat, is a deep inlet with white sand and pinewoods, situated far below and beyond the hilltop town of Sant Miquel. One side of the inlet has been taken over by sleekly modern hotels, but their guests seem to prefer their own swimming pools to Sant Miquel beach.

In addition to walking in the wooded hills, one of the most popular local attractions is the **Cova de Can Marçà**, a cave where sound and light effects enhance the natural wonders of stalagmites and stalactites.

FORMENTERA

Ibiza's tiny neighbor is a world apart. Less than 4 nautical miles away — not half an hour by hydrofoil and only an hour by ferry — the island of Formentera beckons to those seeking a quieter life. It has long sandy beaches as well as easy terrain in the interior for bicycles or scooters. Formentera has no airport, nor are there any plans to build one. It boasts a sizable salt lake but no fresh water. Cisterns, some of them dating from Arab times, catch whatever rain falls from the sky, and supplementary water supplies are shipped in when needed to this desert island.

Grandiose cliff-top views of heavenly Port de Sant Miquel are an irresistible magnet for photographers.

Potential water shortages have not been enough to stop the developers, however, and hotel complexes and scores of new apartment blocks line the beaches of Es Pujols, Mitjorn, Es Caló, and Cala Sahona. These centers attract most of the tourists and summer residents, who swell the permanent population of roughly 5,000 to 20,000 or more. The impact of this seasonal influx of tourists (mainly German, British, and French) has been dramatic. Still, there's room to spare on Formentera.

Constrained by the limited water supply and the absence of an airport, the pace of construction and change has been kept within reasonable bounds. Buildings, for example, are not allowed to rise higher than four stories. Traffic has also been controlled — if you're staying here, a bicycle is the best way to explore an island that measures no more than 20 km (12.5 miles) from end to end, one-fifth the size of Ibiza. For daytrippers, however, the best option is to rent a car, scooter, or moped. Although the island is small, it is too large to see in one day by bicycle. Don't rely on public transport, either, because bus service is extremely limited.

But many visitors prefer to linger in Formentera for more than a day. They're attracted by the sun and sea, by the incomparable beaches, and by some of the finest windsurfing and scuba diving in the Mediterranean. Beautiful sandy beaches (like Platja de Mitjorn) go on for miles. You'll see many nude sunbathers, and toplessness is the order of the day. Nude bathing is officially legal only on the isolated beaches of Illetas and Llevant, but it is practiced virtually everywhere. As a rule, officials leave people free to sunbathe as they please.

For all Formentera's happy-go-lucky ways, traditions are still firmly entrenched. Farmers continue as precariously as ever, scratching a living from the arid, rocky soil. Wheat, barley, and oats are the most significant crops despite the

lack of freshwater sources. Wheat, in fact, has been cultivated since Roman times, when the island was known as "Frumenteria," or "wheat producer." Other crops include the grapes used for Formentera's distinctive dry red wine *(vino de pagés)*. Almond and fig trees thrive, but the olive trees here bear little fruit.

The stark, formidable parish church dominates the center of San Francesc Xavier.

Life still revolves around stucco farmhouses with tiled roofs and columned verandas. Lush, red, juicy tomatoes, threaded together in garlands, hang from the rafters to dry while almonds are shelled and — together with honey and figs — sold to tourists. You'll also find the fruit of an industrious winter's knitting: gloves, scarves, caps, socks, and pullovers fashioned from local, coarse, cream-colored homespun wool. No matter how enthusiastically they welcome tourism, the islanders seem reluctant to abandon a rural lifestyle, which further enhances the local charm.

Island Sights

From Ibiza Town, ferries and hydrofoils heading for Formentera pass two uninhabited islands: Es Vedrà, which hovers like an apparition on the horizon off to the west, and Espalmador, which is popular with yachtsmen for its white-sand beach.

Passengers disembark onto the quayside at **La Sabina**, Formentera's port. From here you can take in at a glance the languorous activity of the harbor and the spate of construction that is changing the skyline of the town. Here, too, you can rent a car, scooter, moped, or bicycle or catch the bus. The port serves as the only terminal for Formentera's limited — and not too reliable — public transport system. There are also taxis available for hire.

Follow the main road inland past the island's lone gas station (which is closed after dark!) to the town of **Sant Francesc Xavier**, known in Castilian as San Francisco Javier. The population of Formentera's chief city has expanded to around 1,000. Parked at the back of the new town hall is the jaunty Land Rover that serves as a fire engine, the first on Formentera and just one of the beneficial side effects of the tourist boom.

Last stop before you drop! Far de la Mola — the "lighthouse at the edge" — with the sea far below.

The most prominent structure here is the 18th-century **Church of Sant Francesc Xavier**. Squat as a bunker, this fortress of whitewashed stone sheltered townspeople when pirate raids threatened. Tourists now descend on the town's three main streets, and a growing number of souvenir shops proclaims the new order of things.

From Sant Francesc, take the road that leads southwest to Cap Berbería (the southernmost point in the Balearic Islands). Just over 1.5 km (1 mile) out of town you pass the turnoff to the small, sandy bay of **Cala Sahona**, which is framed by cliffs of red rock and hotel and holiday apartment blocks. Except for Cala Sahona, this part of the island is sparsely populated. There are a few farms, scattered fields marked by stone walls, and corrals enclosing sheep, goats, and pigs. The parched landscape grows ever more desolate as you approach **Cap Berbería**, and the road deteriorates until it's no more than a dusty track. The cape itself is the haunt of wild goats and the site of an isolated lighthouse and a watchtower, both built high above the sea.

After the solitary beauty of Cap Berbería comes **Platja de Mitjorn**, a sublime arc of sand 8 km (5 miles) long that is popular with summer vacationers. The area has been developed with a number of hotels, notably Club Hotel La Mola (Formentera's most luxurious resort), Hotel Formentera Playa, and the Mar-i-land complex.

Continue east to the village of **Nostra Senyora del Pilar** and on to **Far de la Mola**, an old lighthouse built in 1861 and still in operation. A veteran keeper lives on the premises, tending the beacon that is visible 65 km (40 miles) out to sea. As a nearby monument proclaims, Far de la Mola was featured in the Jules Verne adventure *Journey Round the Solar System.* Time and technological advances have passed the lighthouse by, but it's not difficult to see why it caught

Verne's imagination. Literary connections aside, the site has a certain splendor, providing ravishing views over Formentera and out across the sea.

More glorious still is the panorama from the *mirador* above **Es Caló**, a lookout point that is one of the highest spots on the island. It stands right alongside the road in full view of the narrow spine of land that connects eastern Formentera to the island's western half. The white expanse of Platja de Mitjorn, clearly visible on the southern side, is paralleled by the rocky strip of beach on the Es Caló side. Es Caló's tiny harbor dates from Roman times, when it was Formentera's only port. Nearby, a Roman encampment, **Can Blai**, has recently been excavated. Today Es Caló is yet another target for tourist development, and there are already several small hotels and apartment complexes set among the pinewoods.

After Es Caló, return west along the main trans-island road to **Sant Ferran**, a pleasant village with a pretty church. It had its brief moment of international fame as the rendezvous for American and European hippies. The bar at Fonda Pepe claims to have served drinks to Bob Dylan, and acolytes shared high-flying wisdoms at the nearby grotto of Cueva d'en Jeroni.

Head north back to the coast and **Es Pujols**, Formentera's main resort village. Scores of bars, restaurants, and kiosks cater primarily to German tourists. In peak season near the village, you can scarcely see the sand for all the lounge chairs, sunbaked bodies, *pedalos,* and windsurfing gear. Farther west you can swim in relative seclusion or eat at a simple beach restaurant. Don't expect much in the way of facilities; these simple establishments are intended to be dismantled at the end of every season, when the area returns to blessed tranquility.

The oldest construction on Formentera, a prehistoric stone circle of dolmen megaliths, lies not far from Es Pujols at **Ca Na Costa** (between the La Sabina road and Formentera's salt lake). The site is still under excavation but open to the public. A shelter has been erected to protect the limestone pillars from the elements.

Also here is Formentera's salt-reclaiming area, **Las Salinas**. To reach the salt lake, follow the road on the outskirts of La Sabina before turning right (eastward) down a rough lane, at the end of which you turn left.

Roman times, the salt pans today are the source of 20,000 tons (18,000 metric tons) of salt each year. The salt has large crystals (with a higher density than those from Ibiza) and is considered excellent for curing fish. The export point is, of course, La Sabina, first and last port of call on any round-the-island jaunt.

Formentera's beginnings — a prehistoric circle of dolmen megaliths at Ca Na Costa.

Island Flora

The rewards of a close-up look at the countryside of Ibiza include a botanical treasury. If you're interested in plants and flowers and want to know what's in bloom when, here's a calendar.

January: Mimosa bushes are covered with yellow puffballs.

February: White and pink almond blossoms are unforgettable as a blizzard. On the hills giant blue iris, yellow gorse, and tiny bee orchids create an impressionist landscape.

March–April: Fields of daisies — even daisy bushes — and pink field gladioli announce spring on Ibiza.

May–June: The striking scarlet of flowering pomegranate trees contrasts with the red of poppies in the cornfields and with the bright yellow flowers of the prickly pear.

July–August: Now the garden flowers bloom: honeysuckle in yellow and cream; the blue, trumpet-shaped morning glory; and pink and white oleander. Bougainvillea starts to sprout bright green leaves and scarlet flowers. Even when you're on the beach, there are lingering signs of spring from the white, sweet-scented sea daffodils pushing up out of the sand.

September: Rainbows of petunias, geraniums, and dahlias appear. Look out for the white spikes of the yucca plant.

October: The prickly pear is laden with egg-sized fruit of yellow and purple; tiny narcissus and merendera flower after the first autumn rains. Enjoy the zinnias — brown and yellow.

November: In shady woods, white and pink heather hugs the ground, while rosemary bushes, covered with tiny blue flowers, dot open areas.

December: Orange and lemon trees bear fruit.

And almost the year round in the most unexpected places — in tiny crevices between rocks, alongside every road and path — the wildflowers, sometimes almost microscopic, offer a wild bouquet of color and life.

From almond blossoms to the morning glory's purple bugle, island flora is a joy for nature lovers.

WHAT TO DO

SPORTS AND OUTDOOR ACTIVITIES

Water sports are the natural first choice on two islands that enjoy year-round sunshine and a sea that is almost always temperate. Aquatic life has been enhanced in recent years by the considerable efforts of local authorities to keep coastal waters unpolluted.

But there is more to Ibiza and Formentera than beaches. There are plenty of wilderness trails for hikers, mountain-bikers, and horse riders wishing to explore the interior or the clifftop paths. And there are also limitless opportunities for those who want to relax and do nothing at all. The fine white sands (or smooth pebbles, for those who don't want an occasional breeze blowing a few grains into their hair) make ideal day-beds for lazing in the sun. And as far as lazing goes, some visitors never get around to reading that fat paperback they bought at the airport. The model here is the islands' myriad lizards, who are very happy and have never heard of Stephen King.

Beware the Island Sun!

But active and passive alike must be careful in the Mediterranean sun — and not just during the summer months. The greenhouse effect is now merciless on the islands. You'll get your suntan without working at it, even after only a half hour in the morning and another half hour in late afternoon. Remember that those ultraviolet rays operate even in the shadows, and the sun bounces off the water, the wet rocks, and the white walls. Don't ignore hats, a strong sunscreen, and T-shirts for protection when not swimming.

Watersports

Boating and sailing. The yacht clubs and many of the beach resorts supply sailing boats for hire, and some also have schools. Rates are not at all prohibitive and are often cheaper than in mainland Spanish resorts.

Sailboats. Suitable for a crew of two, these are just the ticket if you want to learn to sail. Beach bars and most water sports schools rent sailboats. Instruction is optional, but lessons are advisable for real novices.

Motorboats. Local officials rigidly enforce the Spanish law stipulating that only captains with an official license may operate motorboats. Consequently, motorboats are seldom available for rent to tourists without a skipper.

Pedalos. These popular two-seat contraptions are powered by a foot-driven waterwheel. They are sufficiently stable for a young child accompanied by an adult. They are also perfect as a personalized ferryboat to reach coves for snorkel-

A windsurfer catches a breeze off Formentera (with Ibiza in the background).

Plain sailing…let the rugged coastline drift by while you catch a tan.

ing or just to avoid the crowds. Pedalos can be rented by the hour. Give yourself plenty of time to return to shore before your rental period has expired.

Windsurfing. This sport has almost completely replaced waterskiing, which is now principally a pastime for people with their own motorboats. Windsurfing is a major attraction on Ibiza and Formentera. Equipment can be rented at windsurfing schools *(escuelas de windsurfing)* as well as many resorts.

Fishing. Catching fish along the rocks of the coastline is a popular pursuit, no matter how unlikely the prospect of a large haul. Offshore, the professional fishing business — once a major source of income in Ibiza — has dwindled significantly. Island fishmongers these days are just as likely to sell frozen fish from afar as the freshly caught local article. A few dogged fishermen still work the banks of Ibiza's Riu de la Santa Eulària, especially at the point where it empties into the sea.

But if you're having a go yourself, don't expect too much more than a nibble. You might have more fun, and even success, "spinning" from the back of a boat; the equipment is easily available and cheap. Catches of brill almost half a meter (18 inches) long are not uncommon in winter.

Scuba diving and snorkeling. It is essential to note that spearfishing with scuba equipment is strictly forbidden. Also, the shores of Ibiza contain so much archaeological treasure that the government keeps a sharp eye on all divers. Before you can dive underwater, you must have a license from the CRIS (Centro de Recuperación y Investigaciones Submarinas, or Underwater Recovery and Research Center). Be forewarned: *violators are prosecuted.*

Scuba diving schools operate on Ibiza and Formentera, though the locations tend to change from year to year. You must apply for your own license; a medical certificate is also required.

Fortunately, the whole family can enjoy a hint of the thrills of undersea swimming. Snorkeling equipment is relatively cheap in the shops, but test the facemask carefully before you buy it. With a little practice, almost anyone can find an interesting rock formation and watch the multicolored fish pass in review. Snorkel fishing with spear guns is legal, but the fish (which can often be frisky with unarmed snorkelers) now know to scatter at the sight of a harpoon.

Nude bathing is more likely to shock fellow tourists than to offend the long-suffering Ibicencos.

If you don't feel squeamish about it, you can prowl the rocks in shallow waters with a facemask and spear in search of squid. These tentacled creatures might look terrible under water, but out in the air they're revealed as small and not dangerous. In winter, thousands of squid lurk among the rocks in very shallow waters along the coast, and the only equipment you need to catch them is a facemask and *gancho* (hook). The problem is learning how to tell the difference between the squid and the rocks they settle in. If you can solve that one, you'll have a lot of fun as well as a few catches.

Swimming. Most Ibiza hotels and apartment complexes offer their own freshwater pools. On Formentera, however, this is not necessarily the case.

Amenities inevitably come hand-in-hand with crowds. On the main beaches be prepared to do battle with lots of other sun seekers, all equally happy to find restaurants, toilets, showers, and changing rooms. Territorial rights, in the form of a deck chair or beach mattress, can be assured for a nominal sum.

The concept of a professional lifeguard is practically unknown on both Ibiza and Formentera. Some beach bars do keep first aid supplies. However, most of the favorite beaches are well protected from waves and undertow, and they have a very gradual slope. Normally they are safe, but be sure to take care on a rough day.

Donkey Treks

More than 50 trained donkeys work at the burro ranch near Santa Gertrudis. An outing from here includes a 20-minute ride over a mountain followed by a wine-tasting party. Watch out for the donkey that drinks *sangría* from a *porrón,* which is quite a feat. The combination of the scenery, the ride, and the general fun and games makes this a very popular excursion. Many travel agencies offer the donkey trek excursions, but if you want to drive to Santa Gertrudis on your own it will cost you about half as much.

Using donkeys for leisure purposes is a recent development. Burros have been used as beasts of burden since the times of the ancient Egyptians. Those big-eared, sure-footed creatures can still be found on farms all over Ibiza, gainfully employed in spite of competition from tractors and trucks.

Sports on Land

For those weary of water, there is plenty to do on land. Once again, however, remember to be careful in the sun.

Tennis. Although there are no grass courts on the islands, a number of asphalt or composition courts are available at hotels and apartment complexes. Courts can be rented by the hour, usually with advance booking. A few hotels offer professional coaching; prices vary greatly according to the reputation of the teacher.

Golf and miniature golf. One unexpected sight, in a remote valley near Cala Llonga, is a meticulously tended, exquisitely green golf course. Those who feel a holiday isn't the same without a game are welcome to tee off there. If you can't get into the golf club, try miniature golf in Sant Antoni, Santa Eulària, or Portinatx on Ibiza, and at Club La Mola on quieter Formentera.

Hiking and mountain biking. These are two ideal ways of getting off the beaten track and away from the madding crowd. The newly environmentally conscious tourist authorities provide a plethora of trail maps and descriptions of the countryside and sights along your route. Trails are signposted with the island's emblem: Eleonora's Falcon. Tourist office brochures for each of Ibiza's five communes — Santa Eulària, Sant Antoni, Sant Josep, Sant Joan and Ibiza Town — grade the trails according to difficulty: (1) slopes perhaps too tough for the elderly; (2) mostly flat, with moderate slopes; (3) almost completely flat and easy for all; (X) unsuitable in some cases for walkers, in others for bikes.

Most sacrosanct of all Ibicenco customs, the siesta should always be respected. Don't telephone or disturb people in the early afternoon hours.

Wear sensible walking shoes and a hat as protection against the sun, and pack drinking water and a flashlight (torch) for the way back from a sunset view. When part of the route coincides with a normal road, remember that pedestrians should walk on the left.

Horseback riding and horse racing. The countryside of Ibiza, with its gentle green hills and grid of back roads, is perfectly suited to horseback riding, an elegant alternative to hiking and biking. You can find stables in the following places: Portinatx, Sant Antoni, Santa Gertrudis, and near Santa Eulària. In addition, there are instructors and horses suited for children.

Horse races are held on Tuesday and Saturday at the Hippodrome Ibiza in Sant Rafel and on Sunday at Sant Jordi

The terracotta ceramics of Sant Rafel have centuries of tradition behind them and make for wonderful souvenirs.

(check with the tourist office for seasonal changes). The trotting races are particularly exciting, and the Hippodrome even stages Roman chariot races.

Hunting and shooting. It's not certain which came first: the famous Ibicenco hounds or the island's craze for weekend hunting forays. In either case, the locals set off into the hills more for the exercise than for the kill. The occasional partridge and rabbit are just about the entire range of possibilities. The hunting season runs from October to February. Clay pigeon shooting is also popular.

Check for details on hunting permits at the local tourist office or write to ICONA, Carrer Sabino de Arana, 22, Barcelona, Spain.

SHOPPING

Shopping hours

Strictly observing the traditional afternoon siesta, shops stay open in Ibiza from around 9am to 1pm and from 4pm to 8pm. During summer some shops remain open for an extra half hour or more in the evening to cope with the crush. Bars and cafés are usually open from as early as 8am — even earlier near the discos — until midnight or later with no break for the siesta. Most boutiques open only during the tourist season, starting at Easter and ending in November.

Sale: ***Rebajas***

Where to shop

The area around the port in Ibiza Town offers the largest choice of shops on the island. Quite a few establishments devote themselves primarily to their local customers, rather than sell just stock tourist gear. The trendier fashion boutiques are to be found both in La Marina and up in Dalt Vila, the latter especially for high-style sandals. Vara de Rey shops cater more to the mass market.

Best Buys

As a rule, prices on Ibiza are slightly higher than on the Spanish peninsula, and you will find few real bargains these days.

Shoes. Ordinary shoes for both men and women can be quite cheap, but anything stylish is likely to cost as much as at home. Very popular are the traditional *alpargatas* or *esperdenyes de bed,* made of local *esparto* straw, hemp, and white *pita* fiber at heel and toe. They are ideal for the beach, for shopping, or for lounging around at the hotel. You'll very likely throw them away by the time you're ready to leave.

A pharmacy or chemist's is called a *farmacia* (fahr-mah-thyah). And they don't sell film, cosmetics, toilet articles, books, or newspapers.

Bags. Another perennial favorite, useful and inexpensive, is the voluminous straw shoulderbag for shopping or carrying beach equipment. Popular with both islanders and visitors, they come in several sizes for children and adults. Over the years these bags have proven so handy that, to keep up with demand, the local supply of genuine handmade bags has been augmented with imported goods.

Jewelry. Gold and silver jewelry made on the spot or elsewhere in Spain is popular for both quality and price. You will also see "hippie" jewelry (mostly Mexican- or Indian-style silver) on sale especially at the markets in Punta Arabí and Sant Carles. Some of the artisans here look as if they're straight out of the 1960s.

Clothing. The trendy resort clothing available here — fashioned on the island by the designers of the Ad-Lib group —

has a cachet all its own. Selling from Manhattan to Tokyo, styles change in detail each season, but the trademark "Ibiza look" remains light and airy, with a full cut and bright colors setting off the basic Ibicenco white. In another category altogether are the hand-knitted and crocheted folkwear made by island women.

Pottery. The terracotta bowls of Sant Rafel and Sant Josep have centuries of tradition behind them. Many of the patterns and forms still show a medieval Arab influence — although craftsmen today might not be prepared to admit it. Be careful what you choose, since inadequately fired, unglazed pottery is risky to ship or pack.

Liquor and tobacco. Both are cheap compared to European and American prices. Prices in town are low. Imported Cuban cigars, plentiful and cheap, are a favorite take-home present although still outlawed by US Customs. While for-

Lines of earthenware vases, urns, bowls, and pots — you name it... they can throw it!

eign-brand alcohol, produced under license in Spain, sells for just a few hundred pesetas a bottle, there are more unusual local spirits that might make apt souvenirs of Ibiza. Such drinks are spiced with the island's wild herbs, resulting in interesting and varied flavors. *Hierbas* (a mixture of herbs), *anís seco* or *anís dulce* (dry or sweet aniseed) and *frigola* (thyme) are just a few heady tipples worth looking for.

Herbs and spices. Bought off the shelf in the local supermarkets, these cost virtually nothing. Take home a bunch of tiny packets of colorful *azafrán* (saffron) and any other dried herbs you fancy. An overpoweringly fragrant shop located in the port area of Ibiza Town seems to stock just about every imaginable spice.

Local foods. A variety of local and Spanish foodstuffs can be transported home with a minimum of fuss and bother, including almonds, olives, olive oil, sausage, cheese, and dried figs. Look for these items in the picturesque open-air market of Sa Penya (Ibiza Town) or, for a wider selection, at the bustling, covered central market in the newer part of town (Carrer d'Extremadura).

Barbecues

A popular excursion organized by tour agencies is the all-you-can-eat-and-drink barbecue outing. You will arrive at a rustic setting where meat is sizzling over glowing coals and unlimited quantities of red wine or *sangría* are waiting to be drunk. Following the feast, a band usually plays music for dancing.

You'll learn to drink wine from a *porrón*, a glass container with a pointed spout from which the liquid arcs through the air into your open mouth — in theory, anyway. To enjoy the experience fully, don't wear your best clothes and remember to put a napkin around your neck.

Antiques. In the past there must have been intriguing opportunities to buy up Ibicenco antiques and ship them home. Today it would take more time scrounging about than the average visitor is willing to invest. Browse around the shops, however, and you might find an appealing piece of old ironwork or handcarving. At the least you will always be able to take home a rusty old door key or two or a kitchen iron of genuine pre-electric vintage.

ENTERTAINMENT

The Folk Culture of Ibiza

In Spain's post-Franco revival of authentic folk culture, Ibicenco folk singing and dancing have become recognized as exuberant art forms that are truly unique to the island. Regular shows take place in villages such as Sant Miquel and Sant Josep. There are often special one-time performances in other towns and villages during fiestas, which usually occur on saints' days and other religious festivals. Making your own way to the villages will cost less than if you take an organized excursion, which includes the inevitable libation of *sangría.*

Disco dancers should check out the islanders' folk dances. Their eroticism is rooted in the lusty sensuality of the ancient Phoenicians.

The colorful traditional costume for men calls for red *barretina* hats, bandannas tied round the neck, gold-trimmed black corduroy or cotton jackets over loose-fitting high-collared white shirts, bright red cummerbunds, baggy trousers of white linen (wide at the thighs but tight at the ankles), and an open, toeless version of the familiar Ibicenco straw *alpargata* shoes.

The costume donned by the women is more lavish. It includes a long, pleated skirt of homespun wool, either black

On saints' days and other religious occasions Ibicencos don lavish traditional dress.

or white; an apron with elaborate patterns; a long-tasseled fine silk shawl over the shoulders; and a big lace mantilla over the head, with hair braided down the back and sometimes tied with a schoolgirl ribbon. Around the neck hang a heavy golden necklace, ribbons, a gold scapular with images of saints on both sides, and a crucifix. Much of this adornment — such as the *emprendad* necklace — is gold filigree of Arab design. In addition, the women wear various heavy rings. The clothing is so original and ornate that a fair amount of time is spent at each folklore show explaining them in detail. Even children on foot or in strollers wear miniature versions of these costumes.

The traditional *ball pagès* (country dances) take many forms, each portraying an often long-forgotten ritual. Most of the dances now performed suggest ancient courtship, with the man being forceful and arrogant, the woman shyly flirtatious. In one dance, the women form a circle, moving in small steps, their eyes cast down, while the men — outside the circle — seek to attract their attention with ostentatious high kicks. Often the songs have witty, ribald lyrics inevitably watered down in the impromptu translation.

The music is played on typically Catalonian — and in some cases uniquely Ibicenco — instruments: wooden flute and small drum (handled together by one man with astonishing dexterity), a sort of steel saber struck rhythmically, and large castanets. The music reflects unmistakable Arab roots, though over the centuries it has accumulated a number of additional elements. Some of the light-hearted songs require the singer to emit an unusual guttural "ye-ye-ye" sound.

Festivals

The popular *fiestas* of Ibiza are less formidable than the equivalent *ferias* of mainland Spain. Now that tourists are a primary audience, several feast days offer special events and fireworks that were never part of the original celebrations. For the visitor, the most interesting observances are the modest old standbys, generally the saint's day of a village: sober religious processions often held by candle light, with folk music and an array of quaint costumes. It is not an uninhibited carnival, but in its own way it is much more memorable.

smokers: *fumadores*
nonsmokers: *no fumadores*

In the following list we describe those annual festivals held on fixed dates. Check with the tourist information office for information about other events.

first Sunday in May *Fiesta Floral* (Santa Eulària): a spring festival combined with a flower show.

23–24 June *St. John the Baptist's Day* (Ibiza Town and Sant Antoni): fireworks, bonfires, craft markets, and festivities. This is an important holiday, when Ibicenco landowners and tenant farmers make their verbal contracts for the coming year on 24 June.

16 July *St. Carmen Maritime Festival* (Ibiza Town): regattas held in honor of the Virgen del Carmen. Similar celebrations are held in Sant Antoni on the following Sunday.

25 July *Fiesta of Santiago* (Formentera): procession, folk songs, and dancing in honor of St. James.

1–8 August *Santa Maria de las Neus/* "Our Lady of the Snows" (Ibiza Town): marching bands, fireworks, folk dances, sporting events, and religious services in honor of the patron saint.

24 August *St. Bartholomew's Day* (Sant Antoni): procession, high mass, concerts, fireworks, and sporting activities.

8 September *Fiesta de Jésus* (Santa Eulària): a popular religious festival.

29 September *St Michael's Day* (Sant Miquel): celebrated with special panache by masterly folk dancers and musicians.

1 November *All Saints Day* (Ibiza and Formentera): special cakes, pastries, and nuts are sold in markets.

3 December *Fiesta in Sant Francesc Xavier* (Formentera): procession, dancing, and folk songs.

Nightlife

Such is the appeal of Ibiza's nightclubs that, after a couple of weeks vacationing on the island, many people manage to leave without a suntan. And no regrets. For some, the nightlife is the only reason to come here in the first place. By day, they sleep — or dance at one of the daytime discos. Some British charter groups have been known simply to fly in for the night and go home the next day. At last estimate Ibiza boasted some 80 clubs and nightspots, ranging from opulent, glowing discothèques (complete with elegant restaurants, multilevel cocktail bars, half a dozen dance floors, and even an indoor swimming pool) to sleazy, somber saloons with just one little dance floor. Both have their *aficionados*. The one thing they have in common is a deafening sound system.

entrance: *entrada*
exit: *salida*

A major island highlight is the extravagant "theme" evening with shows involving audience participation: beauty contests for all sexes, communal baths in foam — or whipped cream — and fashion parades.

For many years Ibiza Town itself was not the place to go for the club scene; instead, it attracted only a special clientele to Dalt Vila's gay bars. Now it boasts two major clubs, the Pacha and Divino (which are considered too refined for some tastes), with plenty of other entertainment available. Sant Antoni can certainly still lay claim to the island's most spectacular clubs, but it also features smaller clubs and bars with disc jockeys or live music of various kinds, including jazz. The Playa d'en Bossa area west of Ibiza Town also has a lively nightlife, with Irish bars, live music, and clubs.

Take in the broad sweep of Playa de ses Figueretes from the castle in Ibiza Town. Then, get ready to party!

In the summer months a Discobus service operates between the major resorts from midnight to dawn (see Recommended Nightclubs, page 143, for details on current hot spots). Don't forget that many large hotels also offer evening activities every night of the week, and you don't need to be a guest of the hotel to participate.

Ibiza Town's casino, handily located on the waterfront promenade (Paseo Juan Carlos I) is open year round. To gain entrance to the gaming room, you must present your passport or identification papers. Then, for a small fee, you will receive a computerized admission card good for one or more days of roulette (both French and American) as well as blackjack and craps. The stakes for many of the games are low, so you can try your hand without risking too much. Early in the evening, tourists crowd in for a look at what's going on, but — as the night progresses — the dyed-in-the-wool gamblers gradually

Ibiza has plenty of activities for children. Getting behind the wheel is where it's at for this junior thrill seeker.

take over. Also on the premises are a nightclub with a floor show and an art gallery.

Most films in Ibiza's cinemas are dubbed into Spanish. Aside from the more conventional cinemas of Ibiza Town, other places that show films on the island are old-fashioned if not picturesque. Either once or twice a week you can see films in English in both Santa Eulària and Sant Antoni.

ACTIVITIES FOR CHILDREN

Children are rarely happier than when playing on a beach. Fortunately, most of the beaches on Ibiza and Formentera provide good facilities for the whole family. The fine white sands of Cala Vedella or Cala Llonga, for instance, are ideal for building castles or simply digging holes.

When that gets boring — and it rarely does — take the kids out on a pedalo or a glass-bottomed boat (particularly at Playa d'es Canar). What they spot below the boat is likely to whet the appetite of some of the older children for snorkeling.

When choosing your hotel, check on the special facilities many provide for children's activities down on the beach or around the swimming pool.

Most of the half-dozen horseback riding stables scattered across the island have ponies for children. Trotting races are great fun for the whole family, especially the Roman chariot races at Sant Rafel. A more leisurely way of getting around is on a donkey from the burro ranch near Santa Gertrudis — with sangría as a bonus for the parents.

The annual summer solstice celebrations of St John the Baptist's Day (23–24 June) offer spectacular fireworks shows. You'll also see fireworks during the week-long Santa Maria de las Neus festival around Ibiza Town's harbor at the beginning of August. Another great fireworks event is St. Bartholomew's Day (24 August) at Sant Antoni.

EATING OUT

The variety of Ibiza's cuisine faithfully reflects the island's image as a cosmopolitan resort with traditions firmly anchored in a Catalan and — even earlier — an Arab past. The French, Italian, and international restaurants (including Chinese and Indian) are of good quality. The local Ibicenco cooking can be both robust and subtle, whether it be with Spanish hams and pork from the mainland or with saffron and other sweet and sour spices from North Africa. Marrying them all are the variations to be created with fish and shellfish caught in local Mediterranean waters or farther afield. And as an unabashed magnet for the mass-tourism market, Ibiza also has plenty of pizzerias and casual spots for fish-and-chips and hamburgers.

If, with a few exceptions, Sant Antoni happily dishes out fast food, Santa Eulària is renowned for the quality of its typical Ibicenco restaurants. Bars for delicious *tapas* — appetizers that combine to make a whole meal — are particularly good not only in Ibiza Town but also out at Santa Gertrudis. One of the main reasons for an excursion on Ibiza is to hunt down one of the many fine restaurants in the interior. Formentera is better known for its seafood taverns on the beach. (See Recommended Restaurants for a selection of the islands' eating establishments.)

RESTAURANTS AND MEAL TIMES

Spanish restaurants are officially graded and then awarded a rating in "forks": from one fork to four. Note, however, that ratings are awarded based on facilities and not on the quality of the food. Several forks might guarantee only higher prices.

Spanish restaurants generally offer a "day's special" *(menú del día)*. This is normally three courses plus wine at a set price. The *menú* proves economical if not inspired, since the law stipulates that the price charged cannot be more than 80 percent of the à la carte sum of its parts. It is important to note that if a waiter asks "*¿Menú?*" he is referring to the special dish of the day. If you want to look at the actual menu and see what else is offered, then you should ask for *la carta*.

Most menu prices include taxes and a service charge, but it's customary to leave a tip if you were served satisfactorily; an appropriate tip is about 10 percent. All restaurants announce that official complaint forms are available to dissatisfied clients.

On the Spanish mainland, late dining hours perplex visitors: lunch hardly ever seems to start until 2pm, and dinner might wait till 10pm. However, on Ibiza the farmer-and-fish-

Ready to eat? Ibiza offers plenty of culinary delights — in a variety of charming settings.

erman tradition rules out late meals. Restaurants serve lunch from 1pm to 3pm and dinner from about 8pm to 11pm.

Here is a useful hint for keeping costs down: ask for *vino de la casa* (house wine). This will cost well under half the price of a brand wine and prove to be of a satisfactory quality. Overall, most drinks are less expensive than in the UK and US.

Breakfast

With lunch and dinner the major island meals, the standard Ibizan breakfast is simply a cup of coffee and a pastry. *Ensaimadas* (sweet rolls made with lard) are a Balearic specialty. In winter you can sample *churros* (sugared fritters), which you dip into coffee or hot chocolate.

In deference to foreign habits, most hotels and some cafés now offer a *desayuno completo* consisting of orange juice, toast, and coffee, either with or without eggs. Breakfast coffee (*café con leche)* is half coffee, half hot milk. Hot chocolate with cream is known as *un suizo,* meaning, not surprisingly, "a Swiss."

"You're welcome."
De nada. **(day nah-dah)**

Beach Restaurants

There has always been a special appeal to beach restaurants serving meals and drinks — or at least a snack — near the water's edge. These modest establishments are set up right on the sand. Because they're supposed to be dismantled at the end of each season, most are somewhat makeshift, but they are nonetheless convenient and appealingly atmospheric.

Bars and Cafés

From early in the morning to late at night, bars and cafés serve breakfast, snacks, coffee, and drinks. At most open-air cafés,

Take a pit-stop at an outdoor café and watch the world go by.

a cup of coffee buys you a ringside seat for as long as you care to linger; no one will rush you. One of the few exceptions is in Sant Antoni, where some cafés refuse to serve coffee at all during peak hours, preferring the higher profits from alcohol.

Wines and spirits are served at all hours in Spain. Children are welcome in most bars and often accompany their parents on late-night outings, having recouped their energy during their siesta.

Bar and café bills include service, but small tips are the custom. It usually costs 20 percent less to sit at the bar for a coffee or a drink than to be served at a table.

Note that *cafeterías* aren't the self-service restaurants that you might recognize. Instead, they are glorified snack bars. The word originally meant a café, but service has been expanded to include full meals.

Bodegas are wine cellars. On the mainland, many popular tourist bars have been designed to re-create the feel of a traditional wine cellar. However, on Ibiza a *bodega* is usually a wholesale and retail wine store rather than a place to sit and try the vintages. Prices are reasonable here.

Tapas bars offer an alternative to a formal meal in a restaurant. A *tapa* is a bite-sized morsel of food: meatballs, olives, fried fish tidbits, shellfish, a vegetable salad — in fact, almost anything edible. The word *tapa* itself is translated as "lid" and derives from the old custom of offering a bite of food along with a drink; the food was served on a saucer sitting on top of the glass, like a lid. Today, sadly, the custom of giving away the *tapa* has gone, though the idea of selling snacks is stronger than ever. You can wander into a *tapas* bar, point to the items you like, and eat your way down the counter, rather like a smorgasbord. One helping is called a *porción;* a large serving is a *ración,* and half as much is a *media-ración.* It pays to learn these terms, as you can easily spend more for *tapas* than for a conventional dinner.

Making a meal of *tapas* is perfectly acceptable — at lunchtime rather than dinner.

WHAT TO EAT

Spanish Specialties

Gazpacho (pronounced "gath-PAT-cho") is an Andalusian invention, a highly flavored, chilled soup to which chopped cucumbers, peppers, tomatoes, onions, and sippets (croutons) are added to taste. Aptly described as "liquid salad," it can be a rousing refresher.

Paëlla ("pie-ALE-ya"), in all likelihood of Arab origin, crossed the sea to Ibiza from Valencia. It is named after the iron pan in which the saffron rice is cooked. Among the additional ingredients are morsels of squid and shrimp, mussels, rabbit, sausage, peppers, chicken, onions, peas and beans, tomatoes, garlic… and whatever else happens to inspire the cook at the moment.

Classically, *paëlla* should be served only at lunchtime and always cooked to order. It takes more than half an hour, time enough to pacify your hunger with another dish for which

Spain is known: *tortilla española* (Spanish omelet), which has no connection with Mexican tortillas. This is less fluffy than a French-style omelet, more like a substantial egg-and-potato pie.

Fish comes in from all over the Mediterranean and is therefore sometimes frozen rather than freshly caught in Ibiza waters. Fish dishes are usually served grilled, accompanied by a salad and fried potatoes. The local "catch of the day" is frequently *pez espada* (swordfish) and comes as a very satisfying grilled steak. Alternatively, try *salmonete* (red mullet), *mero* (grouper), or *lenguado* (sole).

In season you can find delicious varieties of shellfish from *langostinos* (crayfish) to *gambas* (prawns) and *mejillones* (mussels). And don't forget *calamares:* strips of squid, most commonly fried in batter *(a la romana),* making either a snack or a meal in itself.

By the way, a menu's rather grand sounding *filete de pescado a la romana con patatas fritas* is just the correct Spanish way to say "fish and chips."

Squid, Anyone?

If you're out fishing, you might catch a squid — or you might simply buy one at the market and pretend to have caught it! In either case, everyone in sight will congratulate you and advise you how to cook and eat your catch.

Need a recipe? The simplest method is to simmer the squid in its own ink. Otherwise, hang it up on a line until the sun completely dries it out (at least 12 hours), cut it up into very thin slices, grill it over open coals, and then sprinkle it with lemon juice. For something along the same lines but not quite so time consuming, try a dish of *calamares* (deep-fried squid) in a local restaurant.

There's plenty of meat on the menu as well: local pork and lamb, fowl, and game. If you prefer a beefsteak, you can often choose from *chateaubriand, tornedos,* and *entrecôte.* The most tender cut, similar to filet mignon, is called *solomillo (filete).*

Ibizan Specialties

The local cuisine makes much use of olive oil, red wine, cereals, and the island's herbs: fennel, laurel (bay leaves), basil, oregano, thyme, marjoram, and mint. Since Phoenician times, islanders have used the local salt to preserve fish. After Arab irrigation methods enabled the growing of rice, green vegetables, citrus fruits, and saffron, the Catalans brought in the custom of frying in onions, tomatoes, red peppers, and garlic. We list below the descriptions of a sampling of typical dishes.

Sopas: tasty, cheap soups of lentils, rice, butter beans, and green beans — your choice of *sopa de pescado* (fish soup) or *sopa marinera* (seafood soup).

Ibiza's excellent, homegrown fruit and vegetables add color to a local market.

Garbanzos: chickpeas served Ibicenco-style with parsley, oil, and garlic.

Sobrasada: classical Balearic pork sausage, seasoned with sweet peppers.

Butifarrons: spicy black blood sausage.

Sofrit pagès (country stew): this hearty meat-sausage-and-potato dish is properly cooked in a broth of chicken and lamb, with saffron, garlic, sweet pepper, cinnamon, and cloves.

Frita pagesa (country fry): beef, lamb or pork chops, and pork liver fried with garlic, mushrooms, red pepper, and potatoes.

Guisat de peix (fish stew): Ibiza's lusty answer to the French bouillabaisse, an assortment of fish with all the Mediterranean spices, plus a distinctive touch of cinnamon.

Tonyina a l'eivissenca: a tuna delicacy with pine kernels, raisins, eggs, spices, lemon juice, and white wine.

Dulces: sweets, the great Ibiza weakness, from typical Balearic sweet breakfast rolls *(ensaimadas)* to *graixonera,* a kind of bread pudding, and *flaó*, a tart made with fresh goat's cheese and mint. *Macarrones de San Juan* turns out to be macaroni cooked in sweetened milk and cinnamon. *Oreietes* are ear-shaped pies flavored with aniseed.

"Enjoy your meal!"
¡Buen provecho!
(bwayn pro-vaych-oh)

The fresh local fruit is delicious. After a large lunch on a hot day, choose from grapes from the nearby vines — cooling in a bowl of water — or select apricots, figs, peaches, or a ripe melon. In the right season, abandon any weight concerns and enjoy a bowl of fresh strawberries and cream *(fresas con nata),* widely advertised by the island's restaurants and cafés.

WHAT TO DRINK

The most famous of all Spanish wines is, of course, sherry *(vino de Jerez),* a wine fortified with brandy. You will find two principal types: *fino* and *oloroso*. *Fino* is a dry sherry, pale in color with a rich bouquet. *Manzanillas* and *amontillados* belong in this category. Any *fino* will make a good apéritif.

An *oloroso,* on the other hand, is a heavy, dark dessert wine that is sweetened before being sold. Brown and cream sherries are *olorosos,* and so is an *amoroso,* though it's medium dry and pale in color. An *oloroso* is a good after-dinner drink.

For an adequate table wine, try one of the many unpretentious wines that come from mainland Spain or Mallorca. These unsung yet worthy vintages very often cost just a little more than bottled mineral water. In contrast, some of the well-known Spanish wines can be quite expensive but, for many palates, not necessarily of better quality. On rare occasions you might find a restaurant serving *vino de*

Quenching a Thirst

In the Balearic Islands wine is often drunk from a *porrón,* a communal container made of pottery or glass. With its wide mouth and long tapering spout, it looks more like a watering can than a drinking vessel. You fill it at the top and drink the wine from the spout; the stylized shape is traditional. The version for water (which is drunk the same way) is called a *cántaro.* During the heat of the day workmen will pass this around so that everyone present can drink their fill.

The technique isn't easy to master: tilt the container until the liquid flows into your mouth in a stream, and don't touch the spout with your lips or tongue.

Tradition credits the Arabs with its invention. Apparently they were inspired by the Prophet's dictum that wine should not be allowed to touch a Muslim's lips.

pagés (local red wine). Islanders often drink this somewhat acid wine mixed with lemonade *(gaseosa).*

If you're not in the mood for wine with your meal, have no qualms about ordering something else. No one will turn up a snobbish nose if you prefer beer, mineral water, or a soft drink. In fact, at lunchtime even some Ibicencos themselves consider wine off-limits — it's just too relaxing.

Spanish brandy has a less delicate taste than French cognac, and you might find it too heavy or sweet for your liking. It can be very cheap, often the same price as a soft drink. An expensive brand like Carlos I is much smoother.

"Cheers!"
¡A su salud!

Sangría, rather like punch, is a popular thirst-quenching refresher, especially in summer. Made from a mixture of red wine, lemon and orange juice and peel, brandy, and mineral water with ice, it may strike you as too heavy to be consumed with a meal. When you do try *sangría,* make certain it's freshly made.

A word about prices: If you insist on sticking to imported Scotch or bourbon, expect to pay a relative fortune. However, a wide range of familiar liquors and liqueurs are available at very low prices made under license in Spain. A visit to a large liquor store will reveal prices startlingly lower than what you'd pay at home.

Ibiza is proud of its own native liqueurs. The most widely seen is *hierbas* (which means, literally, "herbs"). This sweet and fairly mild potion is usually a homemade product blended with herbs and sold in old bottles. It costs less — and frequently tastes better — in the more remote areas. The syrupy *hierbas* ("YAIR-bus") can be sipped before or after meals. In hot weather, islanders drink it with ice.

Frigola, a sweet digestive drink good with ice, is commercially bottled in Ibiza from formulas using island-grown herbs, mostly thyme. Two aromatic aniseed drinks are also produced locally. Beware, though, since these colorless liquids have a considerable kick. *Anís dulce* is sweet, *anís seco* is dry and dangerously potent. These resemble French *pastis,* Greek *ouzo,* or Turkish *raki.* Ibizans like their *anís* neat (straight). Foreign imbibers, not brought up on this custom, usually prefer to dilute it with a large splash of water. *Palo,* a slightly bitter aniseed drink that is dark brown in color, tastes best in a long tall glass with the addition of gin or soda and ice.

To help you order and for more information on wining and dining in Ibiza, we would recommend you purchase the *Berlitz Spanish–English/English–Spanish Phrase Book and Dictionary* or the *Berlitz European Menu Reader.*

When in Ibiza, start your morning the way the locals do — with a sweet breakfast roll.

To Help You Order...

Could we have a table?	**¿Nos puede dar una mesa?**
Do you have a set menu?	**¿Tiene un menú del día?**
I'd like a/an/some …	**Quisiera …**

beer	**una cerveza**	milk	**leche**
bread	**pan**	mineral water	**agua mineral**
coffee	**un café**	napkin	**una servilleta**
cutlery	**los cubiertos**	salad	**una ensalada**
fish	**pescado**	sandwich	**un bocadillo**
fruit	**fruta**	sugar	**azúcar**
glass	**un vaso**	tea	**un té**
meat	**carne**	(iced) water	**agua (fresca)**
menu	**la carta**	wine	**vino**

...and Read the Menu

albóndigas	**meatballs**	lenguado	**sole**
almejas	**baby clams**	manzana	**apple**
anchoas	**anchovies**	mariscos	**shellfish**
angulas	**baby eels**	mejillones	**mussels**
arroz	**rice**	melocotón	**peach**
atún	**tunny (tuna)**	merluza	**hake**
bacalao	**codfish**	naranja	**orange**
besugo	**sea bream**	pescadilla	**whiting**
entremeses	**hors-d'oeuvre**	queso	**cheese**
caballa	**mackerel**	pimiento	**green pepper**
cerdo	**pork**	piña	**pineapple**
chorizo	**a spicy pork sausage**	plátano	**banana**
		pollo	**chicken**
cordero	**lamb**	postre	**dessert**
dorada	**sea bass**	pulpo	**octopus**
filete	**filet**	salchichón	**salami**
boquerones	**fresh anchovies**	pez espada	**swordfish**

INDEX

HANDY TRAVEL TIPS

An A–Z Summary of Practical Information

ACCOMMODATIONS *(alojamiento)*

Spanish hotel prices are no longer controlled by the government. Accommodations in the Balearic Islands range from the simple but clean rooms in a *pensión* (boarding house) to the more luxurious surroundings of a resort hotel. The majority of visitors to Ibiza favor travel with a package tour, so accommodations will be arranged in advance. But if you're traveling independently, when you check in you will be asked to sign a form indicating the hotel category, room number, and price (which usually includes breakfast). In the off-season, rates are theoretically lower and vacancies are much more numerous.

One of the most popular types of accommodation is a package arrangement consisting of a furnished apartment or villa. The cost is often little more than the scheduled airfare alone, but arrangements usually need to be made well in advance.

a single/double room	**una habitación sencilla/doble**
with bath/shower	**con baño/ducha**
What's the rate per night?	**¿Cuál es el precio por noche?**
Is there a reduction for children?	**¿Hay algún descuento para los niños?**
That's too expensive.	**Eso es demasiado caro.**

AIRPORT *(aeropuerto)*

Both international and domestic flights fly into Ibiza's modern airport. If no luggage carts are available, porters will usually carry your bags the few steps to the taxi rank or bus stop. Souvenir shops, tourist information offices, car rental counters, and currency exchanges operate here, as well as a duty-free shop — no longer applicable to citizens of European Union countries. (Ordinary shops in the towns sell perfume, tobacco, and alcohol

— tax included and at reasonable prices.) Airline buses link the airport with the center of Ibiza Town, a 15-minute drive. There is a year-round bus service every hour from 7:30am until 10:35pm.

Porter!	**¡Mozo!**
Taxi!	**¡Taxi!**
Where's the bus for…?	**¿Dónde está el autobús para…?**

BICYCLE and MOTOR SCOOTER RENTAL *(bicicletas/ scooters de alquiler)*

A practical and fun way to explore the islands is to rent two-wheeled transportation that can cope with even the most narrow and bumpy paths. Bicycles can often be rented from the same places that rent motor scooters and mopeds, but at about one-quarter the price. A driving license is required when renting a Vespa or a mobylette.

Vespas are squat motor scooters with engine capacities of 150 cc to 175 cc, powerful enough to transport driver and passenger with ease. Mobylettes are elementary 49-cc mopeds requiring little mechanical knowledge, and passengers are not permitted, with the maximum speed about 30 km (18.5 miles) per hour. For more adventurous speedsters, Bultaco trail bikes (250 cc) are occasionally available.

The use of crash helmets is compulsory in Spain when driving a motorcycle, whatever the capacity of the engine.

Where can we hire mountain bikes?	**¿Dónde alquilan bicis de montaña?**
I'd like to hire a bicycle.	**Quisiera alquilar una bicicleta.**
What's the charge per day/week?	**¿Cuánto cobran por día/ semana?**

BUDGETING for YOUR TRIP

Because of Ibiza's tourist boom — and because it's an island — certain prices tend to be higher than on mainland Spain. However, the cost of living still remains lower than in many other European countries and in North America.

How much your holiday will cost depends upon your budget and taste, but you really don't need a lot of money to have a good time. Some prices seem topsy-turvy. In a neighborhood bar, soft drinks, beer, and Spanish brandy all cost about the same, but a bottle of mineral water might cost more than a bottle of wine. Generally, the biggest bargains can be found in eating, drinking, and smoking.

To give you an idea of what to expect, here are some average prices in Spanish pesetas. However, they should be regarded as approximate, as inflation creeps relentlessly up. Prices quoted may be subject to a VAT/sales tax (IVA) of either 6 or 12 percent.

Airport transfer. Bus to the center of Ibiza Town 85 ptas. Taxi from the airport to Ibiza Town or vice versa 1,200 ptas.

Babysitters. 1,000 ptas per hour.

Bicycle and moped rental (per day). Bicycles 700 ptas; mopeds 1,500 ptas; motor scooters 2,500–4,000 ptas. You will have to pay a deposit.

Buses (one-way). Ibiza to: Santa Eulària 150 ptas; Sant Antoni 150 ptas; Sant Miquel 165 ptas.

Camping. 500 ptas per person per day.

Car rental (unlimited mileage). *Fiat Uno* 4,200 ptas/day, 30,000 ptas/wk; *Peugeot 205* 7,700 ptas/day, 30,000 ptas/wk; *Ford Escort* 9,500 ptas/day, 50,000 ptas/wk. Add 15 percent tax.

Cigarettes. Spanish brands: 120–150 ptas per packet of 20; imported brands: 200–250 ptas.

Entertainment. Casino 500 ptas (entry is permitted only on production of passport); discothèque 400–2,000 ptas.

Excursions. Bus tour of Ibiza island 2,800 ptas; of Formentera 5,600 ptas; of Ibiza Town by night 1,500 ptas.

Hotels (double room with bath, in season). 4-star 14,000–19,000 ptas; 3-star 8,000–14,000 ptas; 2-star 4,000–9,000 ptas; 1-star 4,000–6,000 ptas.

Meals and drinks. Continental breakfast 400–750 ptas; lunch or dinner 900–3,500 ptas; beer 125–175 ptas; soft drink 150–200 ptas; Spanish brandy 150–225 ptas; *sangría* (1-liter jug) 1,000 ptas.

Shopping. Bread (500 g) 240 ptas; butter (180 g) 320 ptas; beefsteak (500 g) 800–1,200 ptas; instant coffee (200g) 650–850 ptas; wine (1 liter) 150–400 ptas; fruit juice (1 liter) 150 ptas.

Sports. Golf 6,000 ptas green fee per day, 28,000 ptas per week. Horseback riding 1,700 ptas per hour. Tennis 1,000 ptas per hour.

Taxi. There are no meters in taxis, but there are legally agreed prices for set journeys. Details are available from tourist information offices.

C

CAMPING

On Ibiza, you can camp at sites near Sant Antoni (off Ibiza Town road), at Cala Bassa (west of Sant Antoni), Cala Llonga, Punta Arabí, and Es Canar (all of which are near Santa Eulària), and at Cala de Portinatx up on the north coast. Less demanding wanderers set up camp in Ibiza's coastal caves. If you sleep out in the open, don't stay too close to camping and caravan (trailer) sites; police responsible for the campsite might awaken you to check papers.

Camping is prohibited on Formentera.

May we camp here?	**¿Podemos acampar aquí?**
We have a tent/caravan (trailer).	**Tenemos una tienda de camping/una caravana.**

CAR RENTAL *(coches de alquiler)*

Rental car companies in Ibiza handle a wide variety of vehicles; the few automatics that are available are disproportionately expensive. Off-season rates are often lower.

If you do not have a major credit card, general requirements include a refundable cash deposit plus 20 percent of the estimated rental charge paid in advance. There's also a VAT or sales tax on total rental charges. Third-party insurance is automatically included; for an extra fee the customer can have full insurance coverage.

Renting a car for the day usually means from 8am to 8am. Fuel (and traffic fines) are the customer's responsibility. Visitors from overseas should in theory have an International Driving Permit, but American licenses are accepted almost everywhere. European visitors do not need an International Permit if they have a pink European Driving License.

I'd like to rent a car tomorrow.	**Quisiera alquilar un coche para mañana.**
for one day/a week	**por un día/una semana**
Please include full insurance.	**Haga el favor de incluir el seguro a todo riesgo.**

CLIMATE and CLOTHING

Climate. Ibiza is blessed with a relatively mild climate throughout the year. Maximum temperatures in winter, however, can be a bit cooler than in many other Spanish resorts. Even in the summer months (when the weather is at its warmest) the nights can turn chilly, so it's best to go prepared with a sweater or light jacket. Similarly, though rain is the exception rather than the rule in summer, it can catch visitors unaware. A pack-away raincoat or umbrella is a good investment.

Ibiza enjoys a yearly average of 300 days of sunshine with a daily mean of five hours in winter and more than ten hours in summer. Humidity is about 70% most of the year, rising to a high of 85% in August.

Winter package tours are of course cheaper than in summer, and though resorts are much more peaceful, service in winter can suffer. The chart below shows monthly average temperatures for Ibiza.

	J	F	M	A	M	J	J	A	S	O	N	D
Air temperature												
°F	54	53	56	59	63	71	77	79	72	68	61	56
°C	12	12	13	15	17	22	25	26	22	20	16	13
Water temperature												
°F	56	57	57	61	67	71	76	80	73	68	65	61
°C	13	14	14	16	20	21	24	26	22	20	18	16
Days of sunshine												
	26	14	21	15	28	28	27	31	28	19	24	28

Clothing. Given Ibiza's reputation for freewheeling tolerance, it would be surprising if anyone laid down rules. Dress is informal, ranging from discreet to outlandish. On this island, your own taste is the ultimate rule.

When you're packing, don't fail to consider the calendar. In July and August you're unlikely to need anything beyond the lightest summer clothing, day or night. At any other time of year, even when it's blistering hot at midday, you may have to dress warmer for cool night breezes. In the hot weather, cotton is preferable to — and more comfortable than — synthetic fabrics.

On the beach, dressing poses less of a problem. Some people wear nothing at all (there's official nude bathing in certain areas), and many women go topless. When you're walking to or from the beach, shirts or informal dresses are recommended to be worn on top of swimsuits; the same goes for town wear. More sober clothing should, as a matter of courtesy, be worn when visiting churches. Don't go in a swimsuit or shorts.

COMPLAINTS *(reclamaciones)*

Tourism is Spain's leading industry, and the government takes complaints from tourists very seriously.

By law all hotels, campsites, and restaurants must maintain a supply of official complaint forms *(Hoja Oficial de Reclamación/Full Oficial de Reclamació)* accessible to guests. Merely asking for this form is usually enough of a threat to resolve most matters. New legislation has been introduced that greatly strengthens the consumer's hand. Public information offices are being set up, controls carried out, and fallacious information made punishable by law. For a visitor's needs, however, the tourist office or — in really serious cases — the police would normally be able to handle problems or advise you where to go.

CRIME and SAFETY *(crimen; robo)*

Unfortunately, even on a small island like Ibiza there has been an upsurge in petty thievery. In such crowded places as markets, tourists should be on the lookout for pickpockets and bag-snatchers. Don't under any circumstances take any valuables to the beach or leave them open to view in the car.

If you lose something, check first at your hotel desk, then report the loss to the municipal police or *Guardia Civil* (Civil

Guard). If you lose track of a child at a beach, you should first inquire at the nearest beach bar or restaurant. In town, a lost child would most likely be taken to the municipal police station or Civil Guard barracks.

I've lost my wallet/handbag.	**He perdido mi cartera/bolso.**
I want to report a theft.	**Quiero denunciar un robo.**

CUSTOMS and ENTRY REQUIREMENTS

Most visitors — including citizens of the UK, the US, Canada, Ireland, Australia, and New Zealand — require only a valid passport to enter Ibiza. No visa or health certificate is required. If in doubt, check with your travel agent before departure. The entry procedures at Ibiza airport are generally so informal that passports aren't even stamped. You're usually entitled to stay in Spain for up to 90 days. If you expect to remain longer, a Spanish consulate or tourist office can advise you.

The severely uniformed, white-gloved Spanish customs officials may or may not ask you to open your suitcase for inspection. If you are stopped for any reason, honesty and courtesy should help move procedures along quickly.

Duty and exemptions. As Spain is part of the EU, free exchange of goods for personal use is permitted between Ibiza and the UK and Ireland. Duty-free sales have now been discontinued for EU citizens. For residents of non-EU countries, restrictions are as follows.

Australia: 250 cigarettes or 250 g tobacco; 1 liter alcohol; Canada: 200 cigarettes and 50 cigars and 400 g tobacco; 1.14 liters spirits or wine or 8.5 liters beer; New Zealand: 200 cigarettes or 50 cigars or 250 g tobacco; 4.5 liters wine or beer and 1.1 liters spirits; South Africa: 400 cigarettes and 50 cigars and 250 g tobacco; 2 liters wine and 1 liter spirits; US: 200 cigarettes and 100 cigars or a "reasonable amount" of tobacco.

Currency restrictions. Tourists may bring an unlimited amount of Spanish or foreign currency into the country. On departure, however, you must declare any amount beyond the equivalent of 500,000 pesetas. If you plan to carry large sums in and out again, it's wise to declare your currency on arrival as well as on departure.

I've nothing to declare.	**No tengo nada que declarar.**
It's for my personal use.	**Es para mi uso personal.**

DRIVING

To take your car into Spain, you should have either (1) an International Driving Permit, which is not required for most Western European citizens (ask your automobile association), but because it includes text in Spanish it is recommended in case of difficulties with the police as it carries a text in Spanish; or (2) a legalized and certified translation of your driver's license. You must also carry your vehicle's registration papers as well as a Green Card or other document extending your regular insurance policy, making it valid in foreign countries. With the latter insurance document you should also carry a bail bond, usually available from your automobile association or insurance company.

Driving conditions on Ibiza. The rules are the same as in mainland Spain and the rest of the Continent: drive on the right, pass on the left, yield right of way to all vehicles coming from the right. Spanish drivers tend to use their horn when passing. If your car has seat belts, it's obligatory to use them; fines for noncompliance are high.

The roads of Ibiza are still a few years behind the times but quickly improving. Except for the Sant Antoni–Ibiza motorway and other main thoroughfares, they're narrow, twisting, often filled with potholes, and badly signposted. Be warned that such quaint local attractions as horse-drawn carts, donkeys, sheep, and goats can become deadly perils on the road. When passing through villages, drive with extra care.

Other hazards to look out for include loose gravel and sand on the roadway. Give plenty of leeway to motorcycles, scooters, and bicycles. Never pass any vehicle or obstruction without signaling.

Speed limits: 100 km/h (62 mph) or 90 km/h (56 mph) on the open road and 60 km/h (37 mph) in built-up areas. The speed limit for cars towing trailers (caravans) is 80 km/h (50 mph).

Traffic violations. The armed Civil Guard *(Guardia Civil)* patrol the few highways of Ibiza in cars or on powerful motorcycles. Always in pairs, these tough-looking *hombres* are courteous and will stop to help anyone in trouble. They're also severe on lawbreakers. If you receive a fine, you will be expected to pay it on the spot. The most common offenses include passing without directional lights flashing, traveling too close to the car in front, and traveling with a burned-out headlight or taillight. (Spanish law shrewdly requires you to carry a spare bulb at all times.)

Parking. In Ibiza Town, Sant Antoni, and Santa Eulària, the traffic police have become much stricter about parking; cars are either towed to the police pound (behind Avinguda Isidoro Macabich) or clamped and immobilized. To remove the clamp *(cepo)* can be a time-consuming process. With the clamp, a notice is placed on the windshield warning the motorist not to drive because irreparable damage can occur. In the case of both the clamp and towing, a fine must be paid.

Fuel and oil. All service stations are obliged by law to sell each grade of fuel at the same price. Not every station has a choice of fuels at a given time, and it is recommended that you buy only the best grade available. Most rental cars require lead-free fuel.

There are not that many service stations on the island so be sure to start out with plenty of fuel. Gas station hours are completely irregular on weekends and during fiestas (the local publication *Diario de Ibiza* carries a listing of stations that remain open), and motorists may have to go from Santa Eulària to Sant Josep for gas on a Sunday. The local rule is always to fill up on a Friday and before a fiesta, as well as before nightfall in the summer, when usually only one station stays open on the whole island.

Breakdowns. Because of the heavy workload and a shortage of qualified mechanics, repairs can take longer than at home. Spare parts are readily available for Spanish-built cars, but parts for other makes might be very difficult to obtain.

Road signs. Most road signs are the standard pictographs used throughout Europe. However, you might encounter the following written signs:

Aparcamiento	Parking
Atención	Caution
Baches	Potholes
Blandones	Soft shoulders
Bordes deteriorados	Deteriorated road edges
Ceda el paso	Give way (Yield)
Despacio	Slow
Desviación	Diversion (Detour)
Escuela	School
Estacionamiento prohibido/ Prohibido aparcar	No parking

Obras	Road construction
¡Pare!	Stop
Peatones	Pedestrians
Peligro	Danger
Puesto de socorro	First-aid post
Salida de camiones	Truck exit
(International) Driver's License	**carné de conducir (internacional)**
car registration papers	**permiso de circulación**
Green Card	**Carta Verde**
Are we on the right road for … ?	**¿Es ésta la carretera hacia … ?**
Fill the tank, please, with premium.	**Llénelo, por favor, con super.**
Check the oil/tires/battery.	**Por favor, cheque el aceite/los neumáticos/la batería.**
I've had a breakdown.	**Mi coche se ha estropeado.**
There's been an accident.	**Ha habido un accidente.**

Fluid measures

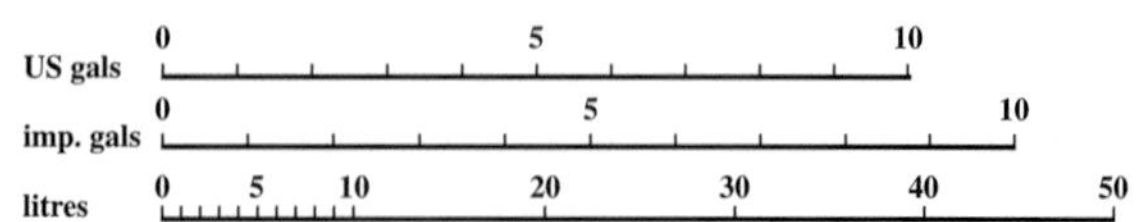

Distance

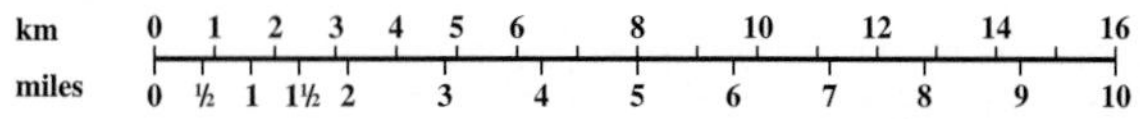

E

ELECTRICITY *(corriente eléctrica)*

Supplies on the islands are either 125-volt or 220-volt AC (50-cycle). To play it safe, ask at your hotel desk. Occasionally, especially when it rains, there is a brief blackout. No one has explained why, but some think it adds to the island's romantic mood. Most hotels supply a candle in every room.

What's the voltage?	**¿Cuál es el voltaje?**
125 or 220?	**ciento veinticinco (125) o doscientos veinte (220)?**
an adapter	**un adaptador**
a battery	**una pila**

EMBASSIES and CONSULATES *(embajadas; consulados)*

Almost all Western European countries have consular offices on Ibiza and Majorca, or in Barcelona. All embassies are located in Madrid. If you run into trouble with the authorities or the police, consult your consulate for advice.

Australian consulate:	Gran Via Carles III 98, Barcelona; Tel. (93) 330 9496.
Irish consulate:	San Miguel 68A, 8th Floor, Palma de Mallorca; Tel. (971) 722-504.
New Zealand consulate:	Traveseria de Gracia 64, Barcelona; Tel. (93) 209 0399.
South African embassy/ consulate:	Edificio Lista, Calle Claudio Coello 91, Madrid; Tel. (91) 536 3780.
UK vice-consulate:	Avinguda Isidoro Macabich 45, Ibiza Town; Tel. (971) 301-818.
US consulate:	Via Laietana 33, Barcelona; Tel. (93) 199-550.

Where's the British/ American consulate?	**¿Dónde está el consulado británico/americano?**
It's very urgent.	**Es muy urgente.**
I need to make an urgent telephone call.	**Necesito hacer una llamada urgente.**

EMERGENCIES *(urgencias)*

If your hotel desk clerk isn't able to help, use the following telephone numbers for urgent situations:

Police emergency	**091**
Ambulance	**301-214**
Fire	**313-030**

G

GAY and LESBIAN TRAVELERS

Spain is a popular place with gay and lesbian travelers, with few places more so than Ibiza. This is truly a place to relax and have hassle-free fun. The island has a host of bars, clubs, cafés, restaurants, and hotels and vacation apartments aimed specifically at gay tourists. A useful web site to consult for local accommodations and activities is <www.respect-holidays.co.uk>.

GETTING THERE

If the choices of travel to the island are bewildering, the complexity of fares and regulations can be downright stupefying. A reliable travel agent who knows the latest fares and specials can suggest which plan is best.

From the UK:

By air. All direct flights to Ibiza's airport from the UK are chartered. If you are not on a charter flight, you can take nonstop scheduled flights to Ibiza from Barcelona or Palma de Mallorca.

Freedom fares offer savings to those who stay 1 day to 1 month, provided you stay over a Saturday night. These fares are ideal if you want to visit several destinations in Spain. Reservations can be changed and stopovers are permitted. **Budget fares** for stays of 1 to 13 weeks in a single destination only (no stopovers, no changes in reservations permitted) are available throughout the year. You must travel in and out on the same day of the week. A 50 percent discount on Budget and Freedom fares is made for children aged 2 through 11. Ask about low "add-on" fares to provincial airports in Great Britain. There are also special low-season money-saver flights for stays of between 1 and 4 weeks (no discount for children).

Fly-drive packages with the use of a car on Ibiza can be obtained with both the Budget and Freedom fares.

Charter flights and package tours (including flight, hotel, and meals) are the most popular ways of visiting Ibiza. British travel agents offer guarantees in case of bankruptcy or cancellation by the hotels or airlines. Most recommend insurance, too, for tourists who are forced to cancel because of illness or accident.

By car ferry and hovercraft. During the summer, when ferry space is at a premium, be sure you have a firm reservation. The principal ferry routes to the Continent are Dover–Calais, Ramsgate–Dunkirk, Newhaven–Dieppe, Weymouth–Cherbourg, Portsmouth–Le Havre, Portsmouth–Cherbourg, and Plymouth–Roscoff. From Ireland, services are Rosslare–Le Havre, Rosslare–Cherbourg, Cork–Le Havre, and Cork–Roscoff. The hovercraft from Dover to Calais takes 35–45 minutes and costs only a little more than the ferry, as does the Seacat catamaran from Dover to Calais and from Folkestone to Boulogne. The driving route from Paris is entirely via toll motorway to Alicante.

There are also long-distance ferries between Portsmouth and Bilbao and between Plymouth and Santander (a 24-hour trip). From Santander follow the N623 to Madrid then the N111 to Valencia or Alicante, or the N240 from Santander to Barcelona.

Car ferries link Ibiza with Barcelona and Valencia as well as with Palma de Mallorca. During the summer months there are also car-ferry services between Denia and Ibiza and between Denia and Formentera, and a weekly ferry between Sète (in the south of France) and Ibiza. Reservations for vehicle space can be difficult to obtain in the high season.

By bus. Express coach services run between London and Barcelona and the Costa Blanca, with frequent departures in summer.

By rail. There are two main routes to Spain from the UK: via Paris and Barcelona (27 hours) and via Paris and Madrid (32 hours). Connections can then be made to Valencia and Alicante. Couchettes and sleepers are available. In addition to the first- and second-class fares, the InterRail Card may be used in Spain by travelers under 26 years of age and the Rail Europe Senior Card by senior citizens. Another fare for those under 26, the Transalpino, is also a bargain.

Eurailpass. Anyone — except residents of Europe — can travel on a flat-rate, unlimited-mileage ticket valid for first-class rail anywhere in western Europe outside Great Britain. The price depends on whether you want to travel for two weeks or longer (up to three months). Either way, you must sign up before you leave home. *Student-railpass* is the same program but for second-class accommodation, available only to full-time students under the age of 26.

From North America:

By air. Direct daily flights to Madrid, with connections to Ibiza, operate from Miami, New York, and Montreal.

Discounted plans include APEX and Excursion fares. Charter flights and package tours are available through airlines as well as travel agents. You'll also find charter flights organized by private organizations, companies, or church groups. The ITX (Inclusive Tour Excursion) lets you book only 7 days ahead for your 7- to 45-day stay. You can pay to extend your stay by up to 45 days. There's also an added fee if you plan additional stops along the way.

GUIDES and INTERPRETERS *(guía; intérprete)*
Local tourist offices can direct you to qualified guides and interpreters and will also inform you of the general price range. In most centers, an English-speaking guide can be hired at short notice.

We'd like an English-speaking guide.	**Queremos un guía que hable inglés.**
I need an English interpreter.	**Necesito un intérprete de inglés.**

H

HEALTH and MEDICAL CARE
The most common cause of illness among tourists on Ibiza is an excess of sun, food, or alcohol — or a combination of all three. The motto to remember is moderation. Do your eyes a favor and wear sunglasses; you have probably never seen the sun reflected so brightly and glaringly off white walls. Use plenty of sunscreen as well.

Note that practically no Ibiza beaches maintain a lifeguard.

Insurance. To be completely prepared, make certain your health insurance policy covers any illness or accident while on vacation. Before leaving home, British citizens should apply at any main post office for form E111, which gives a reciprocal health care agreement between the UK and Spain. Your travel agent can also fix you up with Spanish tourist insurance (ASTES), but it is a slow-moving process. ASTES covers doctor's fees and clinical care in the event of emergency.

Doctors and hospitals. There are doctors in the towns on Ibiza, and their consulting hours are posted. For less serious matters, first-aid personnel (practicantes) can be consulted. Some *practicantes* make daily rounds of the major tourist hotels, just in case. There are a number of outpatient clinics on the island, and one of them operates round the clock in Ibiza Town. In the event of grave emergency, your hotel staff will probably send you there.

Pharmacies/drugstores *(farmacias)* are usually open during shopping hours. After hours, one shop in each town is always on duty for emergencies. Its address is posted daily at all the other outlets.

a dentist	**un dentista**
a doctor	**un médico**
an ambulance	**una ambulancia**
hospital	**hospital**
an upset stomach	**molestias de estómago**
sunstroke	**insolación**
Get a doctor quickly!	**¡Llamen a un médico rápidamente!**

HOLIDAYS

The following holidays are only the national holidays of Spain. There are so many religious, civic or minor holidays celebrated on Ibiza that they seem to come every two weeks. Banks and most shops will close for the day.

With luck, you might be able to help celebrate one of the more colorful local occasions. Since nearly every town is named after a saint, the saint's days take the form of local *fiestas* in the respective places. Ibiza Town lacks a saint's name but not a patron. On 5 August each year, the residents celebrate the feast day of Our Lady of the Snows. (See pages 73–74 for details of *fiestas* that take place in different parts of Ibiza and Formentera.)

1 January	*Año Nuevo*	New Year's Day
6 January	*Reyes (Epifanía)*	Epiphany
19 March	*Día del San José*	St. Joseph's Day
1 May	*Día del Trabajo*	Labor Day
25 July	*Día del Santiago Apóstol*	St. James's Day
15 August	*Asunción*	Assumption
12 October	*Día de la Hispanidad*	Discovery of America Day
1 November	*Todos los Santos*	All Saints' Day
6 December	*Día de la Constitución Española*	Constitution Day
25 December	*Navidad*	Christmas Day

Movable dates:

Jueves Santo	Maundy Thursday
Viernes Santo	Good Friday
Lunes de Pascua	Easter Monday
Corpus Christi	Corpus Christi
Immaculada Concepción	Immaculate Conception

Are you open tomorrow? **¿Está abierto mañana?**

LANGUAGE

Castilian, the national language of Spain, is understood everywhere. However, the islanders customarily communicate among themselves in Ibicenco, derived from the Catalan language. Since Castilian is not the first language for Ibizan residents, they may speak it more slowly than mainland Spaniards do. English, German, and French are useful backup languages in tourist areas. On a brief visit to Ibiza it would be difficult to learn a lot of the local language, although a few words of the Ibicenco dialect will go a long way in producing a smile and friendship. If not, you can always rely on the all-purpose Spanish expression, *"Es igual."* Said with a shrug, it can mean anything from "You're welcome" to "Who cares?"

Ibicenco	*English*	*Castilian*
Bon dia	Good morning	**Buenos días**
Bones tardes	Good afternoon	**Buenas tardes**
Bona nit	Good night	**Buenas noches**
Gràcies	Thank you	**Gracias**
De res	You're welcome	**De nada**
Per favor	Please	**Por favor**
Adéu	Goodbye	**Adiós**

NUMBERS

0	cero	**12**	doce	**31**	treinta y uno
1	uno	**13**	trece	**32**	treinta y dos
2	dos	**14**	catorce	**40**	cuarenta
3	tres	**15**	quince	**50**	cincuenta
4	cuatro	**16**	dieciséis	**60**	sesenta

5	cinco	**17**	diecisiete	**70**	sesenta
6	seis	**18**	dieciocho	**80**	ochenta
7	siete	**19**	diecinueve	**90**	noventa
8	ocho	**20**	veinte	**100**	cien
9	nueve	**21**	veintiuno	**101**	ciento uno
10	diez	**22**	veintidós	**500**	quinientos
11	once	**30**	treinta	**1,000**	mil

The *Berlitz Spanish Phrase Book and Dictionary* covers most situations you're likely to encounter in your travels in Spain. In addition, the *Berlitz Spanish–English/English–Spanish Pocket Dictionary* contains a 12,500-word glossary of each language, plus a menu-reader supplement.

SOME USEFUL EXPRESSIONS

where/when/how	**dónde/cuándo/cómo**
how long/how far	**cuànto tiempo/a qué distancia**
yesterday/today/tomorrow	**ayer/hoy/mañana**
day/week/month/year	**día/semana/mes/año**
left/right	**izquierda/derecha**
up/down	**arriba/bajo**
good/bad	**bueno/malo**
big/small	**grande/pequeño**
cheap/expensive	**barato/caro**
hot/cold	**caliente/frío**
old/new	**viejo/nuevo**
open/closed	**abierto/cerrado**
here/there	**aquí/allí**
free (vacant)/occupied	**libre/ocupado**

early/late	**temprano/tarde**
easy/difficult	**fácil/difícil**
What does this mean?	**¿Qué quiere decir esto?**
Please write it down.	**Por favor, escríbalo.**
Is there an admission charge?	**¿Se debe pagar la entrada?**
I'd like …	**Quisiera …**
Have you something less expensive?	**¿Tiene algo más barato?**
Just a minute.	**Un momento.**
Get a doctor quickly!	**¡Llamen a un médico ràpidamente!**
I'd like film for this camera.	**Quisiera un carrete para esta máquina.**
How long will it take to develop (and print) this film?	**¿Cuánto tardará en revelar (y sacar copias de) este carrete?**
May I take a picture?	**¿Puedo sacar una fotografía?**

LAUNDRY and DRY CLEANING

Most hotels will handle laundry and dry cleaning, but they usually charge more than will a public laundry *(lavandería)* or a dry cleaner *(tintorería)*. You'll find do-it-yourself laundromats in a few areas.

I must have this for tomorrow morning.	**Lo necesito para mañana por la mañana.**

M

MAPS

On Ibiza and Formentera, some places have two names: one Castilian and the other Ibicenco. This often puzzles tourists. To add to the confusion, maps aren't always consistent in their use of place names. With the upsurge in regional consciousness since the death of Franco, place names have become something of a bone of contention here, as elsewhere in Spain, and some Ibiza people would like to see all Castilian place names changed to their Ibicenco equivalents. In towns and villages the words for "street," "square," and so on have been changed from Castilian to Ibicenco, and when new streets are created they are given Ibicenco names.

a street plan of…	**un plano de la ciudad de …**
a road map of the island	**un mapa de carreteras de la isla**

MEDIA

Newspapers and magazines *(periódico; revista).* During the height of the tourist season, all major British and Continental European newspapers are on sale in Ibiza on the evening of their publication day or the following morning. European and US magazines are always available, as is the Paris-based *International Herald Tribune*. For additional news, the local *Ibiza News,* aimed at English-speaking tourists, is published weekly.

If you can read a bit of Spanish, you might also be interested in the daily *Diario de Ibiza,* the local daily.

Do you have any English-language newspapers?	**¿Tienen periódicos en inglés?**

Radio and television. Most hotels have television lounges, but programs are most often broadcast in Spanish. In resorts like Sant Antoni with a large proportion of British visitors, bars have British satellite TV stations broadcasting sports events.

Ibiza's local commercial radio stations have programs in English and German, at least during the summer season, and one station also broadcasts in French and Italian. The BBC and Voice of America are available to travelers with short-wave radios.

MONEY MATTERS

The monetary unit of Spain is the *peseta* (its abbreviated form is written *pta).*

Coins: 1, 5, 10, 25, 50, 100, 200, and 500 pesetas.

Banknotes: 1,000, 2,000, 5,000, and 10,000 pesetas.

A 5 peseta coin is traditionally called a *duro,* so a price quoted as 10 duros means 50 pesetas.

Exchange offices. Outside normal banking hours (see OPENING HOURS), many travel agencies and other businesses displaying a *cambio* sign will change foreign currency into pesetas. The exchange rate is a bit less favorable than in the banks. Both banks and exchange offices pay slightly more for traveler's checks than for cash. Always take your passport with you for identification when you change money.

Credit cards. All the internationally recognized cards are accepted by hotels, restaurants, and businesses in Spain. They are also the quickest way of getting pesetas — from automatic cash distributors.

Traveler's checks. Shops, banks, hotels, and travel agencies in tourist areas accept traveler's checks, though you're likely to get a better exchange rate at a national or regional bank. Remember to carry your passport if you expect to cash a traveler's check. You'll have no problem settling bills or paying for purchases with Eurocheques.

Paying with cash. Although many shops and bars will accept payment in sterling or dollars, you're better off paying in pesetas. Shops will invariably give you less than the bank rate for foreign currency.

Where's the nearest bank/ currency exchange office?	**¿Dónde está el banco/la oficina de cambio más cercana?**

I want to change some pounds/dollars.	**Quiero cambiar unas libras/ unos dólares.**
Do you accept traveler's checks?	**¿Acepta usted checks de viajero?**
Can I pay with this credit card?	**¿Puedo pagar con esta tarjeta de crédito?**

OPENING HOURS

Schedules on Ibiza revolve around the siesta. One of the really great Spanish institutions (though probably inherited from the Arabs), the siesta is most likely aimed at keeping people out of the midday sun. To accommodate the midday pause, most shops and offices are open from 9am to 1pm and then from 4pm to 8pm.

Banks generally open from 8:30am to 2pm, Monday to Friday, and till 12:30pm on Saturday. Post offices open from 9am to 2pm, Monday to Friday, and till noon on Saturday. The main post office in Ibiza Town keeps longer hours: 9am to 1:30pm and 3pm to 8pm.

Restaurants start serving lunch about 1pm, and dinner (earlier here than on the mainland) generally lasts between 8pm and 11pm.

POLICE *(policía)*

Dial **091** for emergency police assistance.

There are three police forces in Spain. The most famous are the *Guardia Civil* (Civil Guard). Each sizeable town also has its *Policía Municipal* (Municipal Police), wearing navy blue uniforms with blue shirts. Members of the third unit, the *Cuerpo Nacional de Policía* (National Police) — a national anticrime unit — wear a navy blue uniform with white shirts. You can call on any one of the three forces (all armed) if you need police assistance. Spanish police are efficient, strict, and courteous to foreign visitors.

Where's the nearest police station?	**¿Dónde està la comisaría màs cercana?**

POST OFFICES

Post offices (correos) are used for mail, telex, and telegrams only. You usually cannot make telephone calls from them. Some post offices limit acceptance of registered mail to certain times. They often stay open a few hours after the normal closing for telegraph business. Mailboxes are yellow with red stripes.

Parcels *(paquetes)* up to 2 kg (4.4 pounds) can be mailed from local post offices. Heavier parcels must be sent from the main post office in Ibiza Town.

If you don't know ahead of time where you'll be staying, you can have your mail addressed to *lista de correos* (Poste Restante or General Delivery) at whichever town is most convenient. For example:

Mr. John Smith
Lista de Correos
Sant Antoni Abad
Ibiza (Baleares)
Spain

Take your passport with you to the post office for identification.

Telegrams *(telegramas).* The main post office in Ibiza Town handles telegrams from 9am to 1:30pm and 3pm to 8pm daily; branches are open only from 9am to 2pm. Your hotel desk will also take care of telegrams for you. Night-letters or night-rate telegrams *(telegrama de noche)* are delivered the following morning and cost less than straight-rate messages.

Have you received any mail for me?	**¿Ha recibido correo para mí?**
A stamp for this letter/ postcard, please.	**Por favor, un sello para esta carta/tarjeta postal.**
express (special delivery)	**urgente**
airmail	**vía aérea**
registered	**certificado**
I want to send a telegram to…	**Quisiera mandar un telegrama a** …

PUBLIC TRANSPORTATION

Bus services. On Ibiza the bus service hasn't quite caught up with the tourist boom. However, tickets are cheap and the crowding just might go under the heading of local color. Private companies link Ibiza with both Sant Antoni and Santa Eulària as well as northern towns. They also operate local runs to beaches. The main lines have a bus every half-hour during summer and sometimes more during busy periods. Even so, tourists have been known to miss the last bus. Note that there's no east – west bus service across the island. To get from Sant Antoni to Santa Eulària, you must change in Ibiza Town. This jaunt takes about 90 minutes. A hitchhiker might do it in 20 minutes. Nightlife enthusiasts should remember the all-night Discobus service.

On Formentera the bus service is irregular and subject to seasonal change; on the whole it is best not to rely on it.

When is the next bus to…?	**¿Cuándo sale el próximo autobús para … ?**
one-way (single)	**ida**
round-trip (return)	**ida y vuelta**

Taxis. The letters *SP* on the front and rear bumpers of a car don't stand for Spain; they mean *servicio público,* and the car is a taxi.

It might also have a green light in the front window and a taxi sign. Whatever it looks like, it's a reasonably economical mode of transport. Some Ibiza taxis have meters but rarely use them, so agree on a price before setting out. The major towns have taxi ranks where the taxis — not the customers — have to line up most of the time.

What's the fare to …	**¿Cuánto es la tarifa a … ?**

Boat services. Ferries link Ibiza with mainland Spain and the south of France (see GETTING THERE). Getting to Formentera is quick and easy from Ibiza: the 17-km (10.5-mile) trip to the port of La Sabina from Ibiza Town takes just over one hour by ferry and 25 minutes by hydrofoil. The journey can be rough, and in adverse conditions the hydrofoils are canceled. Service is frequent during high season but reduced at other times. There are also hydrofoil services to Majorca (a 2-hour trip) as well as numerous boat excursions around Ibiza itself. The frequency of boat service increases considerably in high season (1 July–30 September). You can get more detailed information by contacting your travel agent.

RELIGION

The national religion of Spain is Roman Catholicism. On Ibiza, mass is said in no fewer than 33 different Catholic churches, many of them historic edifices. In summer, notices of masses in foreign languages are posted outside major churches in Sant Antoni and Santa Eulària. Protestant services are also held. Look for notices on hotel bulletin boards. There is no Jewish congregation on Ibiza.

What time is mass/ the service?	**¿A qué hora es la misa/ el servicio?**
Is it in English?	**¿Es en inglés?**

T

TELEPHONE *(teléfono)*
The international code for Spain is **34** with **9** recently added to precede each area code. Thus, for Ibiza and Formentera, the area code is **9 71**. To dial a number in the islands from abroad, dial 34 + 971 + the six-digit local telephone number.

To reach other areas of Spain from Ibiza, dial **9** then the appropriate area code (Madrid is 1; Barcelona is 3; Valencia is 6) followed by the local number.

Although Ibiza's automatic dialing system allows you to dial numbers throughout Spain, it might sometimes be impossible to reach a number across town.

Electronic telephone cards are increasingly available. For coin-phones, line up coins of 5, 25, and 100 pesetas on the ledge before dialing. Unused coins will be returned.

Overseas calls can be made from your hotel (the most expensive way), or more cheaply from telephone offices or call boxes. If you don't have a phone card, be sure to have enough change to complete your call, as these public telephones have no numbers and the other party cannot ring you back. For international direct dialing, pick up the receiver, wait for the dial tone, then dial 00, then the country code, city code, and local number.

To reverse the charges, ask for "*Cobro revertido.*" For a personal (person-to-person) call, specify "*Persona a persona.*"

To find a telephone number for Ibiza Town in the island directory, look under the town's Ibicenco name: Eivissa.

E-mail. Your laptop will need a Spanish modem-adapter plug to link up to the local telephone.

Fax. Most hotels have fax facilities. Be sure to get written proof that the fax has been sent and received.

Can you get me this number in …?	**¿Puede communicarme con este número en …?**

TIME ZONES

Ibiza sets its clocks to Spanish time, which is the same in nearly all the countries of Western Europe: Greenwich Mean Time + 1. In summer, clocks are put one hour ahead (GMT + 2). But the major time difference is in the mind. Punctuality isn't a Spanish — or Ibicenco — virtue.

The following chart shows times in winter:

New York	London	**Ibiza**	Sydney	Auckland
6am	11am	**noon**	10pm	midnight

What time is it?	**¿Qué hora es?**

TIPPING

A service charge is normally included in your restaurant or hotel bill, so tipping is not obligatory. However, it's appropriate to tip bellboys, filling-station attendants, and others for their service. The following chart gives some suggestions:

Hotel porter (per bag)	minimum 50 ptas
Maid	100–200 ptas
Lavatory attendant	25–50 ptas
Waiter	5 percent–10 percent
Taxi driver	10 percent
Hairstylist/barber	10 percent
Tour guide	10 percent

TOILETS *(servicios)*

There are many expressions for "toilets" in Spanish: *aseos, servicios, WC, water,* and *retretes.* The first two terms are the most common.

Public conveniences on Ibiza are as rare as snowstorms. However, just about every bar and restaurant has a toilet for public use. It would be considered polite to buy a cup of coffee or a glass of wine if you drop in specifically to use the facilities.

Where are the toilets? **¿Dónde estàn los servicios?**

TOURIST INFORMATION *(información turística)*

Spanish National Tourist Offices are maintained in many countries throughout the world:

UK. 22 – 23 Manchester Square, London W1M 5AP; Tel. (0171) 486-8077.

US. *New York:* 666 Fifth Ave., New York NY 10103; Tel. (212) 265-8822.
Chicago: 845 N. Michigan Ave., Suite 915, Chicago IL 60611; Tel. (312) 642-1992.
Los Angeles: 8383 Wilshire Blvd., Suite 960, Beverly Hills CA 90211; Tel. (213) 658-7188.

Canada. 2 Bloor St. West, 34th Floor, Toronto, Ont M4W 3E2; Tel. (416) 961-3131.

These offices can supply you with a wide range of colorful and informative brochures and maps in English on the various towns and regions in Spain, as well as information about accommodations and prices.

On the islands themselves, Ibiza Town has a tourist information branch office at Vara de Rey, 13 (Tel. 971/301-900). It is open from 8:30am to 1pm, Monday to Friday, and 8:30am to noon on Saturday. The office responsible for the whole island is at Historiador Josè Clapès 4, Ibiza Town (Tel. 971/302-490; fax 971/302-262).

Where's the tourist office? **¿Dónde està la oficina de turismo?**

W

WEB SITES about IBIZA

You can learn much about Ibiza and the other Balearic Islands on the Internet, including information on hotels, attractions, sports, restaurants, entertainment, and even the current weather. Check out the commercial sites at <www.ibiza-online.com> and <www.ibiza-info.com>. The Spanish government maintains a tourism site for the Balearic Islands at <www.caib.es>. Search engines such as Excite, Looksmart, and Yahoo! will find additional travel-oriented sites if you enter the term "Ibiza."

WEIGHTS and MEASURES

Spain uses the metric system.

Length

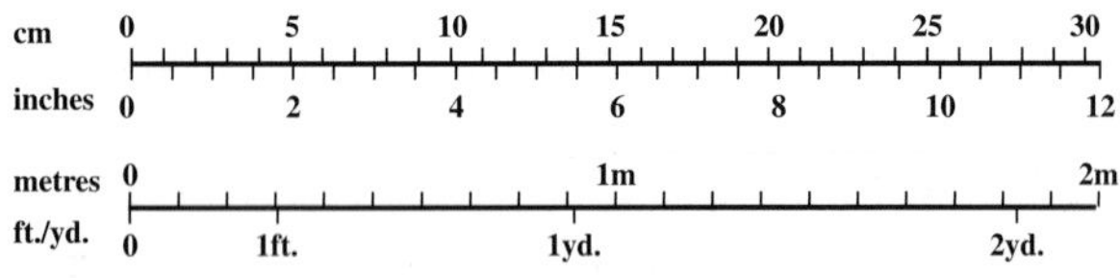

Weight

grams	0	100	200	300	400	500	600	700	800	900	1kg
ounces	0	4	8	12	1lb	20	24	28	2lb		

Temperature

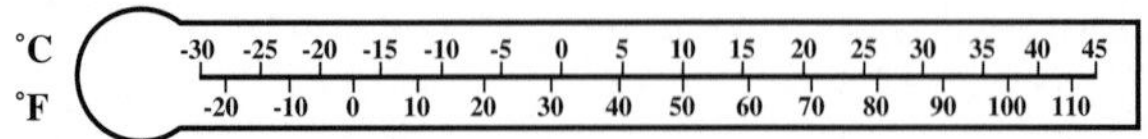

Recommended Hotels

Our selection lists hotels in and around the major resorts (Ibiza Town, Sant Antoni, and Santa Eulària), plus a couple of addresses in the areas of Sant Miquel and Sant Josep. We then list accommodations on the island of Formentera.

The Spanish tourism authorities allot stars to hotels according to complex technical criteria that do not always correspond to price or even to degree of comfort. The island's hotels have three basic categories: *casas de huéspedes* (boarding houses, also known as *pensións* or *fondas*); *hostals* (family hotels, officially allotted one, two, or three stars); and higher-classed hotels (ranging officially from two to five stars).

In some establishments, not all rooms will be provided with private bath. You should be sure to check about this when making your reservation. Rates for rooms with shared bath will be lower.

Except in the simplest accommodations, your nightly room charge includes breakfast and perhaps additional meals. Again, check with the establishment.

Details of hotels with access to the handicapped are available from the organization RADAR (12 City Forum, 250 City Rd., London, EC1V 8AF, United Kingdom; Tel. 0171/250-3227).

In addition to the official government star ratings, we indicate price categories representing the average high-season daily rate for a double room with bath (including 15 percent service charge). However, rates can vary greatly according to the deal struck with your travel agency or tour operator. Note that the more modest hotels and pensions might not accept credit cards; you might be asked to pay in advance.

$$$	over 16,000 pesetas
$$	10,000–16,000 pesetas
$	under 10,000 pesetas

Ibiza Town

Algarb (3 stars) **$$** *Playa d'en Bossa; Tel. (971) 301-716; fax (971) 301-904.* Mammoth modern hotel right on beach, 3 km (2 miles) from Ibiza Town center. 408 rooms.

Cenit (2 stars) **$$** *Archiduque Luis Salvador; Tel. (971) 301-404.* Nicely kept hotel in Puig des Molins quarter near Figueretas beach. Beautiful harbor view from terrace. 62 rooms.

El Corsario (2 stars) **$$** *Poniente 5; Tel. (971) 393-212; fax (971) 391-953.* Tastefully transformed pirate house up in Dalt Vila, popular with artists and writers since the 1960s, with Ibicenco décor, antique fittings, and a grand terrace view over old town and port. 14 rooms.

Don Quijote (2 stars) **$** *Pais Basc 10; Tel. (971) 301-869; fax (971) 341-358.* Large economy hotel near Figueretas beach. 106 rooms.

Mare Nostrum (2 stars) **$** *Pedro Matutes Noguera; Tel. (971) 302-662.* Big (and big-value) economy beach hotel. All amenities: parking, playground, nursery, hairdresser, shops, garden, convention hall, tennis, squash, miniature golf, and pool. 528 rooms.

La Marina (1 star) **$** *Andenes del Puerto 4; Tel. (971) 310-172.* Older waterfront building renovated in 1991, not quiet but with great views of boats coming in and out of port. 25 rooms.

Los Molinos (4 stars) **$$$** *Ramón Muntaner 60; Tel. (971) 302-250; fax (971) 302-504.* Very comfortable hotel in convenient location at Figueretas beach, with pleasant garden, terrace, and pool overlooking sea. 147 rooms.

Montesol (1 star) **$** *Vara de Rey 2; Tel. (971) 310-161; fax (971) 310-162.* Popular spot recently renovated in heart of the Sa Penya harbor quarter, close to Dalt Vila and a one-minute walk from port. 55 rooms.

Ocean Drive (4 stars) **$$$** *Playa de Talamanca, Apdo. 223; Tel. (971) 318-112; fax 312-228; e-mail: odrive@step.es.* Sophisticated, modern design and furnishings. On yacht harbor with view of Dalt Vila; a quick walk from major night clubs. Fine seafood restaurant. 42 rooms.

El Palacio (2 stars) **$$$** *Conquista 2; Tel. (971) 301-478; fax (971) 391-581; Web site: www.elpalacio.com; e-mail: etienne@ctv.es.* Flashy Swiss-operated hotel in an old, renovated Dalt Vila mansion, with cinematic theme (7 suites and rooms with movie-star names and décor) and a parking lot (a rarity in the old-town district).

Parque (1 star) **$** *Vicente Cuervo 3; Tel. (971) 301-358.* Modest but clean, centrally located on corner of Vara de Rey. 29 rooms.

Ripoll (1 star) **$** *Vicente Cuervo 14; Tel. (971) 314-275.* Friendly atmosphere in a small boarding house. 15 rooms.

Sol y Brisa (1 star) **$** *Bartolomé Vicenç Ramón 15; Tel. (971) 310-818.* Modest but immaculately clean and bright little boarding house, two minutes from the harbor. 20 rooms.

Torre del Mar (4 stars) **$$$** *Playa d'en Bossa; Tel. (971) 303-050; fax (971) 304-060.* Luxurious hotel on beach just 1 km (0.6 mile) from town center, set in beautiful gardens with indoor and outdoor pools, sauna, and a much-admired restaurant. 217 rooms.

Tres Carabelas (3 stars) **$$** *Playa d'en Bossa; Tel. (971) 302-416.* Popular hotel in scenic location at beach, offering all modern conveniences including pool, tennis courts, gym, sauna, miniature golf, and garden terrace. 245 rooms.

La Ventana (2 stars) **$$$** *Sa Carrossa 13; Tel. (971) 390-857; fax (971) 390-145.* Fine value and comfort on picturesque little square in old Dalt Vila, with upper rooms and terrace commanding superb view over harbor. Good restaurant. 13 rooms.

Sant Antoni

Arenal (3 stars) **$$$** *Dr. Fleming 16; Tel. (971) 340-112; fax (971) 342-965.* Clean, well-run, well-equipped modern hotel on the east side of harbor on a very popular beach, an easy walk to shops. 131 rooms.

Bergantin (3 stars) **$$** *Playa s'Estanyol; Tel. (971) 341-461.* Large, modern hotel with attractive seafront location. 253 rooms.

Es Plá (3 stars) **$** *Portmany; Tel. (971) 341-154; fax (971) 340-452.* Big hotel with modern facilities, without a sea view but located in pleasant grounds 200 m (220 yd) from beach and a three-minute walk from town center.

Florencio (2 stars) **$** *Soledad 38; Tel. (971) 340-723.* This modest but clean hotel has cheerful service and a convenient location not far from town center. 104 rooms.

Gran Sol (2 stars) **$$** *Soledad 55; Tel. (971) 341-106; fax (971) 341-267.* Large and comfortable modern hotel away from most of the bustle at northeast corner of town, right on Calo des Moro beach. 138 rooms.

March (1 star) **$** *Portmany 10; Tel. (971) 340-062.* Delightful, modestly priced family hotel with exceptionally friendly service and a pool. 86 rooms.

Milord I (3 stars) **$$** *Sant Antoni; Tel. (971) 340-612; fax (971) 340-966.* For details, see Milord II. 153 rooms.

Milord II Fiesta (4 stars) **$$** *Sant Antoni; Tel. (971) 341-227; fax (971) 340-966.* Sister hotels Milord I and Milord II stand together fairly isolated across the bay from town of Sant Antoni. They share fine facilities, including nightly music, two pools, and access to several beaches with good water sports. 218 rooms.

Mitjorn (1 star) **$** *Carrer del Faro 10; Tel. (971) 340-902.* Small, well-kept boarding house close to the port, with view of bay from upper floors. 18 rooms.

Norte (2 stars) **$** *Barcelona 7; Tel. (971) 340-127.* Pleasant boarding house in center of town, a five-minute walk from harbor. Garden and pool. 56 rooms.

Osiris (2 stars) **$$** *Carrer Pino 1; Tel. (971) 340-916.* Comfortable medium-sized hotel, efficiently run in convenient location. 97 rooms.

Palmyra (3 stars) **$$$** *Dr. Fleming; Tel. (971) 340-354; fax (971) 312-964.* Handsome, modern hotel with attractive palm-shaded terrace, nicely located on beach about 1 km (about half a mile) from center of town. First-class water sports and other facilities. 160 rooms.

Pike's (4 stars) **$$$** *Sa Vorera; Tel. (971) 342-222; fax (971) 342-312; Web site: www.ibiza-hotels.com/pikes; e-mail: pikes@ctv.es.* True luxury in this lovingly renovated 15th-century farmhouse tucked away in beautiful countryside but within easy reach of the sea. Traditional Ibicenco décor in all rooms, swimming pool, tennis, minature golf, and VIP card for free access to all major discos. 27 rooms, 22 suites.

San Remo (3 stars) **$$** *Playa de S'Estanyol; Tel. (971) 341-150; fax (971) 341-123.* Right on S'Estanyol beach at Sant Antoni Bay, 3 km (under 2 miles) from town center. Every modern sports facility, nighttime musical entertainment, special attention for children. 147 rooms.

Torres (2 stars) **$** *Soledad 34; Tel. (971) 340-215.* Clean, well-maintained family boarding house not too far from beach. 52 rooms.

Santa Eulària

Las Arenas (2 stars) **$** *Playa es Canar; Tel. (971) 330-790.* Overlooking the sea, with simple but clean and comfortable rooms. 20 rooms.

La Cala (3 stars) **$$** *San Jaime 76; Tel. (971) 330-009; fax (971) 331-512.* Comfortable hotel centrally located by the port and promenade, with garden and swimming pool. 180 rooms.

Cala Nova Playa (3 stars) **$$** *Playa Cala Nova; Tel. (971) 330-300; fax (971) 332-410.* Clean, well-run large hotel 5 km (3.1 miles) north of Santa Eulària and just 50 m (55 yd) from Es Canar beach. Modern facilities include disco. 305 rooms.

Club Cala Blanca (3 stars) **$$$** *Playa Figueral, San Carlos; Tel (971) 335-100; fax (971) 335-040.* **Club Cala Verde** *Tel. (971) 335-111; fax (971) 335-061.* These twin facilities combine in a large, ultra-modern resort complex with handsome gardens, offering complete water sports and other activities on curving Figueral Bay. 320 rooms (Club Cala Blanca); 257 rooms (Club Cala Verde).

Don Carlos (3 stars) **$$** *Urbanización Siesta; Tel. (971) 330-128; fax (971) 330-634.* On quiet beach just 2 km (1.2 miles) from town center, with good water sports facilities and pleasant beach bar. 168 rooms.

Fenicia (3 stars) **$$$** *Urbanización Siesta; Tel. (971) 330-101, fax (971) 330-245.* Handsome, well-appointed hotel in charming gardens, 200 m (220 yd) from sea, with pool, tennis, and miniature golf. 191 rooms.

Los Loros (3 stars) **$$$** *Cas Capita; Tel. (971) 330-761; fax 339-542.* High-quality comfort in big seafront hotel with spectacular view over rocky coast, a short walk from town center. 262 rooms.

Mayol (2 stars) **$** *Algemesi 2; Tel. (971) 330-282.* Modest, clean boarding house a short walk from beach. 17 rooms.

Mediterraneo (2 stars) **$** *Pintor Vizcai 1; Tel. (971) 330-015; fax (971) 339-344.* Bargain-priced family hotel in upper town, with garden, swimming pool, and splendid views of bay and countryside. 63 rooms.

Perla (2 stars) **$** *Playa es Canar; Tel. (971) 331-167.* Small boarding house with pleasant terrace, conveniently located near bus stop. 30 rooms.

Punta Arabi (2 stars) **$$$** *Punta Arabi (Es Canar); Tel. (971) 330-152; fax (971) 339-167.* A hotel attached to large Club Arabi resort complex. Close to beaches, with two swimming pools, disco, and every imaginable sports facility. 72 bungalows and rooms.

Rey (2 stars) **$** *San José 17; Tel. (971) 330-210.* Clean, well-run family boarding house, within easy reach of beach and town center's Plaza de España. 20 rooms.

San Marino (4 stars) **$$$** *Ricardo Curtoys Gotarredona 1; Tel. (971) 330-316; fax (971) 339-076.* Grand, luxuriously appointed modern hotel in heart of town center but only two minutes from sea. 44 apartment-style rooms.

Ses Estaques (3 stars) **$** *Playa Ses Estaques; Tel. (971) 330-200; fax (971) 330-486.* Smart, modern four-story hotel popular with package-tour operators but run with personal touch by local husband-wife team. 159 rooms.

Tres Torres (4 stars) **$$$** *Paseo Maritimo, Ses Estaques; Tel. (971) 330-326; fax (971) 332-085.* Recently renovated modern luxury hotel near yacht marina and beach, with first-rate water sports facilities, tennis, and disco. 112 rooms.

Sant Josep

Les Jardins de Palerm (3 stars) **$$$** *Apartado 62, 07080 Sant Josep; Tel. (971) 800-318; fax (971) 800-453; e-mail: jpalerm@ctv.es.* Haven of tranquillity in tastefully restored 17th-century country mansion near village of Sant Josep, south of Sant Antoni Bay. Swimming pool set amid exquisite flower gardens. 14 rooms.

Sant Miquel

Hacienda (5 stars) **$$$** *Na Xamena, Sant Miquel; Tel. (971) 334-500; fax (971) 334-514; e-mail: htl.hacienda@vic.servi-*

com.es. Ibiza's only five-star hotel, stunningly set in beautiful hillside location with magnificent views of sea and cliffs. Traditional Ibicenco décor in all rooms. All facilities first class; superb restaurants. 52 rooms, 9 suites.

Formentera

Agua Clara (1 star) **$$** *Carretera a Platja de Mitjorn, Ca Mari; Tel. (971) 328-183.* Well-kept hotel on sprawling Mitjorn beach on south coast. 25 rooms.

Bahia (1 star) **$** *Puerto de la Sabina; Tel. (971) 322-142.* Functional hotel right at island's bustling main port. 39 rooms.

Bellavista (2 stars) **$$** *Puerto de la Sabina; Tel./fax (971) 322-255.* Good boarding house recently renovated, with friendly service and spacious restaurant and harborside terrace. 42 rooms.

Cala Sahona (3 stars) **$$$** *Cala Sahona; Tel./fax (971) 322-010.* Well-equipped, modern family hotel, recently expanded, directly overlooking attractive Cala Sahona beach on west coast. Swimming pool and tennis courts. 116 rooms.

Casbah Migjorn (2 stars) **$** *Platja de Mitjorn; Tel./fax (971) 322-051.* Comfortable seafront hotel on Mitjorn beach. 29 rooms.

Club La Mola (4 stars) **$$$** *Platja de Mitjorn; Tel. (971) 327-069; fax (971) 320-050.* In spectacular setting on Mitjorn beach at foot of La Mola cliffs. Recently built luxury resort complex with state-of-the-art water sports, tennis, and miniature golf facilities. 328 rooms.

Club Punta Prima (3 stars) **$$$** *Punta Prima; Tel. (971) 328-244; fax (971) 328-128.* Newly built on promontory at east end of Es Pujols beach on north coast. Bungalows set in lovely flowering gardens, swimming poool, tennis, children's playground, and shopping center. 94 rooms.

Costa Azul (1 star) **$** *Ca Mari, Platja de Mitjorn; Tel. (971) 328-024.* A good-quality, low-budget boarding house at water's edge. Fine seafood restaurant. 13 rooms.

Illes Pitiusas (1 star) **$** *Carretera La Sabina-La Mola, San Fernando; Tel. (971) 328-189.* Modest, recently renovated hotel with friendly service. 26 rooms.

Lago Playa (1 star) **$** *Playa de Levante; Tel. (971) 328-507.* Well-maintained little boarding house on coast just west of Sabina port. Swimming pool. 26 rooms.

Llana (1 star) **$** *Sant Francesc; Tel. (971) 322-205.* Cheerful and clean, this small boarding house in island's main village has a popular restaurant on ground floor. 8 rooms.

Pepe (1 star) **$** *Mayor 68, Sant Ferran; Tel. (971) 328-033.* An inland village rendezvous popular since the (perhaps legendary) visit of Bob Dylan. Frequented by the hippie crowd, this boarding house has friendly atmosphere, 1960s memorabilia, and a good seafood restaurant. 36 rooms.

Rafalet (1 star) **$** *Es Calo; Tel./fax (971) 327-016.* Charming boarding house, clean and well kept, splendidly situated with restaurant and café terrace on tiny natural harbor. 15 rooms.

Sa Roqueta (1 star) **$** *Playa de Levante; Tel. (971) 328-506.* Beachfront boarding house on small, quiet bay west of Sabina port. Good restaurant. 33 rooms.

Recommended Restaurants

We group the following restaurants by major towns and resort areas. Many establishments are situated out of town but easily accessible by rented car or taxi. For out-of-town addresses without street names, we follow the local island convention of naming the highway (for example, Carretera Sant Joan) with — wherever possible — the distance in kilometers measured from its Ibiza Town starting point.

The listing features not only traditional Ibicenco and Spanish national cuisine but also a few "international" restaurants specializing in French, Italian, Chinese, and even Indian food. In rare cases where telephone numbers are not given, reservations are not required. In addition, we let you discover for yourself the countless bars offering delicious tapas snacks, and the ever-changing beach establishments for which telephone reservations are rarely possible.

The following price categories are based on a three-course meal for two, excluding wine. Drinks will of course add significantly to the final bill.

$$$	over 9,000 pesetas
$$	6,000–9,000 pesetas
$	under 6,000 pesetas

Ibiza Town

Antonio $ *Abad y Laserra 21; Tel. (971) 300-577.* Simple cooking. Very popular with local townspeople.

La Brasa $$ *Pere Sala 3; Tel. (971) 301-202.* Good seafood and grills served in quiet oasis in busy quarter, with charming patio and pretty garden terrace right underneath ramparts.

Ca N'Alfredo $$ *Vara de Rey 16; Tel. (971) 311-274.* Terrace or indoor dining on city's handsome esplanade. Robust portions of classical Spanish food.

Celler Balearev $$ *Ignacio Wallis 18; Tel. (971) 301-031.* On broad avenue running north of Vara de Rey. Traditional Ibicenco dishes *(paëlla* a specialty) as well as international cuisine. Wine-cellar décor complete with old barrels.

Chez Françoise $$ *Plaza del Parque; Tel. (971) 391-919.* On charming little square behind Vara de Rey. French-Belgian cuisine.

El Cigarral $$ *Frare Vicent Nicolau 9; Tel. (971) 311-246.* Classical Spanish dishes — good beef and especially fine wines — much appreciated by local connoisseurs. North side of town.

Dalt Vila $$ *Plaza de Vila; Tel. (971) 305-524.* Pleasant terrace dining in old-town square. Mediterranean cuisine with Italian specialties.

El Faro $$ *Garija 4; Tel. (971) 317-578.* Portside restaurant with garden terrace. Known for its absolutely fresh fish kept in water tank, outstanding *paëlla de mariscos* and pasta *paëlla.*

Formentera $$ *Palau 4 (Puerto de Eivissa); Tel. (971) 311-024.* Long-established institution in old fishermen's house facing the harbor. Traditional Ibicenco and international cuisine.

La Masía d'en Sord $ *Carretera Sant Miquel; Tel. (971) 310-228.* Enchanting 17th-century farmhouse with romantic outdoor terrace and appropriately rustic indoor dining; huge house divided into smaller rooms for greater intimacy. Mediterranean cuisine, with salmon a specialty.

Mesón de Paco $$ *Bartolomé Roselló 15; Tel. (971) 314-224.* Attractive country-style décor, tiled walls, carved wood furnishings. Best of Ibicenco cooking, with a truly robust *paëlla.*

Nanking $ *Del Mar 8; Tel. (971) 191-144.* Chinese Cantonese cooking popular with islanders in and out of season.

La Oliva $$ *Santa Cruz 2; Tel. (971) 305-752.* Up in lively quarter of old town, where French and German chefs produce fine Provençal cuisine with Ibicenco touch: grilled seafood, duck with figs in sherry sauce.

El Olivo $$$ *Plaza de Vila 7; Tel. (971) 300-680.* Renowned old-town address with elegant terrace, for sophisticated combination of French and Spanish cuisine.

El Portalón $$ *Plaza des Desamparats 1–2; Tel. (971) 303-901.* Right inside ramparts beside main entrance. Fine restaurant with immaculate and friendly service, famous for its seafood salads and *calamares alla plancha y helado* (hot and cold squid).

S'Anfora $$$ *Bartolomé Roselló 13; Tel. (971) 314-226.* Much appreciated by townspeople for its refined cooking (seafood a specialty) in an elegant setting.

S'Oficina $$$ *Avenida d'España 6; Tel. (971) 300-016.* Ibicencos flock here for Basque cuisine on shady terrace in town center, not far from Vara de Rey. Huge tanks of lobsters and shellfish as well as first-rate meat dishes.

Sa Caldera $$$ *Bisbe Padre Huix 19; Tel. (971) 306-416.* House specialty is the *caldereta de langosta* (pot-cooked lobster). Pleasant, refined setting away from port, behind Santa Cruz Church.

San Juan $ *Montgrí 8; Tel. (971) 310-763.* Tiny place where locals mix with tourists, sharing each other's tables. Basic, robust cooking at bargain prices.

Sausalito $$$ *Plaza de Sa Riba; Tel. (971) 310-116.* At far end of quay, the flagship restaurant of Sa Penya quarter, at once elegant and casual. Excellent Mediterranean cuisine with always-fresh seafood.

El Vegetariano Cártago $ *Punica 8; Tel. (971) 300-942.* Rare vegetarian restaurant , with good quality vegetable pâtés and salads. Open only weekdays at lunchtime.

Victoria $ *Riambau.* No point in telephoning: just try your luck in this ever-popular, always cheerful little place serving traditional food between the port and Vara de Rey.

Sant Antoni

Can Pujol $$ *Port des Torrent; Tel. (971) 341-407.* At water's edge, this renowned seafood restaurant has real fishing-port atmosphere and terrace right on the beach. Fish freshly caught by owner; specialty is fish in garlic cream sauce.

The Curry House $ *Bartolomé.* Catering to mostly British clientèle nostalgic for spicy Indian cooking. Oven-baked tandoori specialties.

Grill Magon $$ *Valencia 23, Port des Torrent; Tel. (971) 340-298.* Nicely prepared grilled steak and seafood brought in fresh from nearby fishing harbor.

Mesón Asturiano $$ *Carretera Sant Antoni, km 12.5; Tel. (971) 347-531.* Traditional Asturian cooking from northern Spain in pleasant family restaurant. The cider is a regional specialty.

Pay Pay $ *Cala Gració; Tel. (971) 340-552.* Despite its name, this is an inexpensive Chinese restaurant where the cooking is much better than the view.

Es Pi d'Or $$$ *Carretera Cala Gració; Tel. (971) 342-872.* Lobster and other seafood specialties from Galicia in elegant, quiet setting.

Rias Baixas $$$ *Ignacio Riquer 4; Tel. (971) 340-484.* Tucked away in old town. First-rate cooking of seafood in both traditional Galician and Basque styles, with a rather kitsch, rustic décor.

S'Olivar $$$ *San Mateo 5; Tel. (971) 340-010.* Century-old olive tree still grows in center of restaurant, but main attraction remains fine classical Spanish and Ibicenco cuisines.

Sa Capella $$$ *Capella de Can Bassora, Cami de Cas Ramons; Tel. (971) 340-057.* Classical Spanish cuisine in elegant setting of an old village church just outside Sant Antoni.

Sa Prensa $$ *Mariano Riquer 9; Tel. (971) 341-670.* Quiet, clean little restaurant serving traditional Mediterranean cuisine in setting celebrating island's rich variety of flora.

San Telmo $$ *Sa Drassana 6; Tel. (971) 310-922.* In narrow cul-de-sac off Plaza d'Antoni Riquer, back from port crowds. Classical Spanish and international cuisine.

Sa Clau $ *Paseo de las Fuentes; Tel. (971) 342-556.* Bustling atmosphere for classical Chinese Cantonese cooking.

Zaifiro $ *San Agustin 118, Port des Torrent; Tel. (971) 343-903.* Great soups and simple Spanish fare popular with local community. Good, cheap set menu.

Santa Eulària

Ama Lur $$$ *Carretera Sant Miquel, km 23; Tel. (971) 314-554.* First-class Basque cuisine in refined setting at this recently renovated traditional *finca* (farmhouse).

Andaluza $ *Sant Vicent 51; Tel. (971) 339-156.* Succulent tapas-style meals in old Andalusian tradition. Specialty is *pescaito frito* (fried whitebait).

Brasserie Dédé $ *Sant Vicent 25; Tel. (971) 332-210.* Cheerful little garden terrace for fresh seafood.

Ca Na Ribes $ *San Jaime 67; Tel. (971) 330-006.* Good Ibicenco specialties (fresh fish and grilled steaks), with bar in garden.

Can Gali $$$ *Carretera Sant Joan, km 12.3; Tel. (971) 332-916.* Superbly prepared Ibicenco seafood specialties and grilled meats served in a house festooned with flowers.

Can Pau $$$ *Carretera Sant Miquel, km 8; Tel. (971) 197-007.* Lovingly restored country house serving authentic Ibicenco dishes, with equally refined service and décor.

Celler Ca'n Pere $$$ *San Jaime 73; Tel. (971) 330-056.* Reputedly the oldest restaurant in Santa Eulària. Traditional setting for classical local specialties and remarkably good wines.

Doña Margarita $$$ *Paseo Marítimo; Tel. (971) 330-655.* Enjoy splendid terrace views over yachting harbor while sampling from wide range of Mediterranean cuisine.

Es Timoner $$ *Puerto Marítimo; Tel. (971) 331-723.* Waterside restaurant with small terrace overlooking yachting harbor. Freshest of fresh seafood and excellent Ibicenco lamb, too.

La Villa $ *San Vicente 3; Tel. (971) 319-074.* Vegetarian breakfast, lunch, and dinner (cocktails served as well) in garden with a light New Age touch.

Sant Rafel

El Clodenis $$ *Plaza de la Iglesia; Tel. (971) 198-545.* "Le Clos Denis" to its Francophile clientèle. Tasty Provençal cuisine in traditional old country house with garden patio.

Las Dos Lunas $ *Carretera Sant Antoni, km 6.* Located just outside of town. Classical Italian dishes, good pasta.

Sant Gertrudis

Can Costa $ *Plaza de la Iglesia; Tel. (971) 197-021.* More *tapas* bar than restaurant, this veritable institution is frequented by numerous aficionados drawn to its arcaded terrace. Delicious snacks *(boccadillos),* sandwiches, and fresh slices from hams hanging from ceiling.

Can Pau $$ *Carretera Sant Miquel; Tel. (971) 197-007.* Outstanding traditional Ibicenco dishes in elegant farmhouse.

La Plaza $$$ *Plaza de la Iglesia; Tel. (971) 197-075.* An enchanting tree-shaded courtyard. Refined, authentic French cuisine with charming service.

Sant Josep

Can Domingo de Can Botja $$$ *Carretera Sant Josep, km 9.8; Tel. (971) 800-184.* Refined combinations of Ibicenco and "nouvelle" cuisine in a handsome country house outside town.

Cana Joana $$$ *Carretera Sant Josep, km 10; Tel. (971) 800-158.* Imaginative and versatile Mediterranean cuisine, primarily

French and Catalan. A tranquil, elegantly decorated farmhouse setting well away from cross-island highway.

Sa Soca $ *Carretera Sant Josep–Sant Antoni; Tel. (971) 341-620.* Large portions of traditional Spanish dishes served on a flowery, shady terrace.

Victor $$ *Carretera Sant Josep, km 7.5; Tel. (971) 800-006.* A large, colorfully decorated garden with an inventive menu (including vegetarian selections).

Sant Joan

Can Gall $$$ *Carretera Sant Joan, km 11.6, San Lorenzo; Tel. (971) 325-055.* Farmhouse restaurant offering classical Ibicenco food and an extensive wine list. Charming and friendly service.

Es Caliu $$ *Carretera Sant Joan, km 10.8; Tel. (971) 325-075.* Truly rustic garden setting beside a windmill. Authentic Ibicenco cooking.

Es Porrons $$ *Carretera Sant Joan, km 12; Tel. (971) 325-151.* Traditional Mediterranean cuisine in farmhouse restaurant with centuries-old carob tree dominating the garden terrace.

Formentera

Casa Rafal $ *Sant Francesc; Tel. (971) 322-205.* Bargain prices for simple rustic cooking in modest setting at center of village.

Es Muli de Sal $$$ *Playa de Ses Illetes.* The yachting fraternity arrives here in outboard dinghies, but other clients also welcome. Seafood dishes served on terrace with superb view of neighboring isle of S'Espalmador and the Ibiza coast.

Recommended Nightclubs

Ibiza's nightlife can be evanescent, with certain clubs open one season and closed the next. We list here only the half-dozen most solidly established top nightspots. You can also explore the scores of others that come and go with the flashy inconstancy of shooting stars but have the special appeal of being often much more outrageous than the island's "institutions."

The half-hourly "Discobus" service (Tel. 971/192-456) runs from midnight to 6:30am between Ibiza Town, Sant Antoni, and Santa Eulària and the beach resorts of the main hotels: Playa d'en Bossa, Port des Torrent, and Es Canar. Beware of going out on the town too early: At many of the clubs, nothing "happens" before 2am.

All these nightclubs are expensive: 3,000–5,000 pesetas (per person) to enter, plus at least 1,200 pesetas for each drink.

Amnesia *Carretera Sant Antoni, km 6; Tel. (971) 191-041.* Huge disco built around an old country house just outside Sant Rafel, a maze of gardens, bars, passageways and mezzanines. Holds 5,000 customers (mostly in their 20s and early 30s), with a casual, non-élitist atmosphere. The crowd is in various states of dress and undress. Famous for introducing the giant foam-bath pool (whipped cream, too).

El Divino *Paseo Marítimo, Ibiza Nueva; Tel. (971) 190 -176.* On the yachting harbor, linked to Sa Penya quarter by motorboat shuttle. A select, smaller night club for relatively more mature clientele. Magnificent terrace provides bewitching view of town at night. Claims Jack Nicholson and King Juan Carlos among its revelers. Refined dining in the restaurant, starting the night "early" around midnight.

Es Paradis Terrenal *Dr. Fleming, Sant Antoni; Tel. (971) 346-600.* Spectacular, with perhaps the island's most beautiful décor: colonnades festooned with plants and vines. Caters to partygoers in their 30s, at first glance sophisticated, but capable of sustaining music turned up to an ear-splitting decibel level and ultimately willing to be sprayed with water toward the end of the night.

Pacha *Avenida 8 de Agosta, Ibiza Town; Tel. (971) 313-612.* Housed in a remodeled old Ibicenco mansion, this is the island's best-known disco, going strong since the 1970s. For many years it has held the reins as the most elegant and fashionable (though by no means the biggest). With four dance floors, countless bars, and a smart restaurant. Specializes in "theme" evenings and fashion shows.

Privilege *Carretera Sant Antoni, Urbanización Sant Rafel; Tel. (971) 198-160.* Replaces the legendary Ku. A deliberately outrageous carnival atmosphere, catering in extravagant but playful manner to all sexes and every variation. Restaurant open 10pm–3am, 15 bars, swimming pool with fountains, gigantic dance floors, capacity up to 8,000.

Space *Playa d'en Bossa; Tel. (971) 396-794.* For the after-after-hours crowd. Opens its airport road warehouse location about 6am or 7am — when others are closing — and continues well into the afternoon. Its slogan is "Happy people in the morning!" Dancers in cages, with techno music going full blast.